WARI

CW00422241

To Carol and Trevor
with very best wishes
from Brent.

WARRIORS

A powerful weight management and fitness programme for men

Robert Paterson

PIATKUS

Copyright © 2001 by Robert Paterson

First published in 2001 by
Judy Piatkus (Publishers) Limited
5 Windmill Street
London W1T 2JA
e-mail: info@piatkus.co.uk

The moral right of the author has been asserted

A catalogue record for this book is available from the British Library

ISBN 0 7499 2166 8

Design by Design 23

This book has been printed on paper manufactured with respect for the
environment using wood from managed sustainable resources

Typeset by Action Publishing Technology, Gloucester
Printed and bound in Great Britain by MPG Books, Bodmin, Cornwall

Contents

Acknowledgements

There are many people whom I would like to thank, both for helping me during the time that this book was written and for being good guides in my life, which have led me to the insights that are this book.

Anne Owen of Sheppard Moscow who through kindness and understanding opened my eyes to a better way of life. Clive Hall who has always been a source of inspiration and a mine of information – a loyal friend through some difficult times. George Metcalfe a superb coach and mentor who gave me some wonderful tips on how to get through writer's nerves. Moya de Wet for her guidance and support in the early days, when I had so much to learn about nutrition. My Warriors team, especially Jacqueline Boorman and Matt Barker who gave generously of their time and expertise in helping me with the Nutrition and Exercise sections of this book. Steve Trew without whose encouragement and support I may never have got back on a bike and competed in triathlons. The Family Heart Association for giving me the opportunity to work with them on the Great Bike Hikes, leading up to the main challenge in the summer of 2001. This has enabled me to keep my focus and literally walk the talk. All the team there, especially Elizabeth Jordan, Joanne Rasor and Michael Livingston for making these events possible. Rachel Winning, at Piatkus Books, who made the process of writing my first book so much easier that it might otherwise have been. Her patience and understanding, as well as guidance and encouragement, were a source of great comfort. AnnA Rushton who has woven a magic spell around this book. Without her support and constant help I would have found the process of writing a daunting task – thank you for making it a rich and enlightening experience. And last, but very far from least, Suely Kennedy, my partner: without her love, patience, loyal support, encouragement and understanding this book would not have been possible – thank you for always being there for me when I needed you.

Introduction

In 1997 I had just returned from Havana where I was working as an international banker. Before that I had been managing director of a Czech Bank in Prague. I was in London looking for a new job in the finance sector, and I had two big problems.

First, I had been working outside London's Square Mile for some time. Second, I had a serious weight problem. I weighed over 22 stone (or 140kg).

Other factors seemed to be against me. The financial institutions were at that time shedding emerging market specialists like me; my age, late forties, was a factor; and my size and shape were the final nail in the coffin. My chances of finding another job were slim, and I knew it.

Worse, my weight had a devastating effect on my morale and self-confidence. If anything was going to undermine my efforts in obtaining another job, a poor mental attitude would be first on the list. It was, however, the only factor that was within my control.

There is a stigma around a person with a weight problem. Those who are overweight are regarded by society as people who cannot cope – possibly lazy and certainly lacking in self-respect. Often that is untrue, but the perception still stands.

I felt both anger and shame when I recognised that, on a shortlist of three candidates for the same job, I would be passed over. To top it all, for my height, 5ft 10in (1.78m), my doctor informed me I was 'grossly obese'. That was a shock; it was a brutal affront. I felt ashamed at how low I had allowed myself to sink. I also realised that I was taking some considerable risks with my health, perhaps even my life. Incredibly, I was exceptionally lucky not to have any serious medical problems related to my weight, but I knew that I was dicing with death and that sooner or later it would catch up with me. Reality was staring me in the face – I had to take action. The plan I came up with was so successful for me that I felt I wanted to share it with other men who are overweight. That is why I decided to write this book.

The Background

My weight first became an issue when I was 8 and went to prep school in Scotland. There, I adopted King Henry VIII as a role model. He was somebody with authority, big and strong, who commanded respect and considerable presence, and I clung to that idea to help me deal with being completely miserable at school.

It was a tough school, designed to forge 'characters' and send the sons of the middle classes to run the Empire. They decided that 'Fat Pat' was not part of the school's image and that I must lose some weight. Teasing became part of daily life. I remember when boiled sweets were given out on Wednesdays and Saturdays, I couldn't have any. I was overweight and the whole school knew about it. I can remember feeling isolated and ostracised. It was the first time in my life that I started to lose weight, on a deliberate diet provided by the school.

Unfortunately, because dieting was not something that I wanted to do for myself, as soon as I was released on holiday I would eat without restriction. That was what I wanted to do. It set up a pattern that lasted right through my adult life.

Over the years I tried most weight-loss regimes and invariably I would lose weight. But the moment I stopped the diet, the weight would be straight back, very rapidly and with interest. Knowing that the weight could be lost, but not kept off, was the real starting point for devising the Warriors programme. Back in 1997 I sat down and thought about the whole idea very carefully.

The Birth of the Warriors Programme

My initial thoughts concerned the pain of those diet periods. They require considerable discipline, substantial energy and a lot of focus. In most cases this is followed by the ignominy of regression – putting the weight on again and more! This is, for most people, an intolerable process.

Praise and compliments are showered upon you as weight comes off, only to be followed by ridicule when it goes back on. This is a classic pattern for many people with a weight issue and I decided there had to be a better way. If you have been through this process, I am sure you will agree. If not, then you are fortunate to be coming to this programme as a first timer, and you will not have to go looking for the holy grail of diets because you will find it right here. The answers to the problem are all inside you, while I, as your guide, will help you build the model that will ensure your success.

The learning curve

My key focus became not just how to get weight off, but how to *keep* it off. I needed to learn something from the past. I had tried so many methods and I knew they all worked, but I just couldn't get them to last. I had to learn from those experiences. I started researching and thinking very carefully about the things that made not just me, but anybody, overweight. I came up with the Big Four of genetics, nutrition, exercise and mindset (these are looked at in detail in Chapter 1).

Putting it together

Now that I had identified the four factors that contributed to weight gain, I was ready to think about how to develop a strategy. I was now much clearer as to where the issues of overweight could arise. Before, I only looked at diets that were designed to shed weight; no one ever talked about keeping the weight *off*. Indeed, even today, few really focus on keeping it off. It may appear cynical to suggest that the weight management industry thrives on repeat business, but that is the reality. Long-term successes are rare. As a result the Warriors programme is not about quick fixes, or short-term weight loss.

The objective of the Warriors programme is to help you lose weight, certainly, but also to treat it as a stepping stone to something much greater, that is, *keeping the weight off*. Furthermore it is about adopting a healthy lifestyle that gives you the opportunity to reach your own goals and objectives. When you are fit you perform better mentally as well as physically. The Warriors programme will help you build your own *unique* formula for fitness and weight management, using skills you already possess from your business life. You bring those skills to bear in such a way that only one question remains:

Do you really want to succeed or not?

This is one of the main differences between Warriors and other weight management programmes. You will realise that you have eminently transferable skills as a manager, which you can apply to resolve your weight management issue. When you follow the Warriors programme, using these skills, you will no longer have to kid yourself about some magic formula – you have the skills, the issues are clear, the choice is yours as to whether you want to succeed or not!

In the past, I found I would go for either a nutrition-based diet or, alternatively, an exercise-based regime. It had never occurred to me in my earlier dieting attempts that I might need to come to terms with a genetic issue or think about my mind-set and my emotional attitude towards food.

When I realised a long-term weight management programme had to combine mind-set, exercise and nutrition, all together in one coherent strategy, the Warriors programme began to take shape.

The Dream Ticket

First I considered what, if time and money were no object, would I do to resolve these issues – what was my dream ticket? I was looking for a remedy similar to the Monopoly card, Get out of Jail Free – for that is how I felt, at 22 stone, a prisoner inside my own body, longing to step out into freedom.

I imagined somewhere warm and sunny, near the sea, with a villa, close to the beach. There I would put the perfect team around me: a nutritionist/cook who would cater for all my dietary requirements; a psychotherapist who would deal with the mind-set issues for me; and a personal trainer, for fitness. I would also need a physiotherapist or a masseur to revitalise a fatigued body.

This process of education, change and transformation would take perhaps a minimum of six months, maybe a year, living in a cocooned world, isolated from friends and society. But two things militated against putting this dream plan into action. One was obviously financial, and the other was that I realised that I would not actually be coping with the whole issue. It might enable me to achieve my objectives in terms of weight management, but I wasn't living a full and 'normal' life, with all its pressures and temptations. What I had to do was face the challenges of day-to-day living. Like a warrior I had to go into battle, at some stage. Training was all very well, but the acid test was living out the idea, in practice.

Finding the Answer

Given that my dream was unrealistic, I embarked upon a campaign of enquiry. Time and again the response was that I could find all the things I wanted, at a cost, but never under one roof. In the absence of a solution, I took the example of a top athlete who surrounds himself with a team to help him achieve his goals and objectives, and did the same for myself. I recruited a State Registered Dietitian, a personal trainer and a lifestyle coach, who worked at focusing me to look forward towards my long-term goals and objectives, rather than trying to sort out any past issues.

Working with a professionally qualified dream team, uniquely focused on my needs, began to give me the understanding I required. When I first started physical exercise I wanted to lose weight – that was the immediate first step. I used a professional personal trainer at my local gym (Courtneys). He gave me a weights and aerobic programme to follow, and encouraged me to try road running. For triathlons

I engaged Steve Trew, who coaches the British junior team. He got me cycling around London.

On the mind-set side I first worked with an American who helped me build up a Food and Mood diary (see Chapter 3). He focused particularly on the 'mood' side, helping me recognise when I was eating through boredom, stress or habit. Later on I worked with a coach who looked at my goals and objectives in all areas, not just food and exercise. That gave me a fresh outlook on how I divided up my work and leisure time. This is something that I am still working hard to balance!

The final member of my dream team was the dietitian, with whom I went supermarket shopping, to get first-hand experience of reading food labels. I started to undertake the discipline of menu planning and preparing food for the week ahead. It was thoroughly tedious and very time-consuming at first, but I did learn a lot from this process.

After three months of working with the dietitian, I was well able to cope for myself and had even befriended food. I began to realise that I could actually enjoy great food, but without putting on weight. I became known to my friends as the low-calorie, low-fat Master Chef. A whole new area of fun and creativity had been discovered and I enjoyed the process immensely (for a selection of low-fat, low-calorie recipes see the cookbooks in the Further Reading, page 195).

Slowly, I started losing weight. I was strongly advised not to shed more than 1 per cent of my body weight per week. That was the maximum healthy recommended weight loss, based on research carried out by the American Heart Foundation, and I tried to stick with that, as best I could.

I weighed myself every day and I measured my calorific intake. To me, those were important disciplines. I required very strong initial control, because I had reached a stage where my eating patterns had gone totally wild and out of control and I needed to bring back some form of order. In the end it took me just over a year to reach my target weight.

Your Supporters

To continue the analogy of the top athlete, to complete your 'dream team', you have your own 'supporters' too, your wife or your partner, family and close friends and the people who work closely with you. You need to make sure that your 'team' is on side, and that they know what you want to achieve, so that they can genuinely support you in your efforts. You know, from your experience of running a business, that people often feel uncomfortable when you try out new systems and make sweeping changes – that is when you need to communicate most, to carry your team with you. The process of weight management is very similar. Handling a successful culture change could be one of the key elements to your success.

Setting Up the Warriors Programme

I realised that I had developed a new way of life with my weight management programme. And it was one I enjoyed because the more the process went on, the more I understood about it, and the more I began to realise that my long-term goals were actually achievable. I didn't have to go back to some ghastly discipline of dieting. I could really enjoy life. I had my eyes open and there was an understanding that had not been there before.

I believe that I can genuinely help others in the process of weight management too. Once you understand the process, which is having a strategy in all three areas of weight management that work in harmony and within a unique formula that is yours, it becomes so much easier. With that ease of understanding comes the skill and through that the mastery of the subject, and every chance of long-term success.

This programme is specially designed for businessmen and executives who have many of the skills to succeed in a weight management programme, but have not yet understood fully how the process works. This may be because it has never been put in familiar language, or because no other programme has

7

been designed so uniquely for men, using their skills and addressing their issues. The Warriors programme turns the body into a business. Weight management is put into language that executives can both understand and relate to.

What is Your Dream?

This is the fundamental question for you to answer. What are the reasons behind trying to lose weight – for you? And it's really the reasons behind it that are going to give you the answers, because losing weight by itself is not going to get you very far. What losing weight might do is to get you into better health if you're not in good health now. What it might do is to enable you to achieve certain things, like playing a better round of golf or being able to walk the dog more comfortably than you can do at present. It's moving yourself towards those goals, by finding the real reason why you want to lose weight that really drives you forward. The body is only a vehicle, but that vehicle needs to be in good condition for you to be able to do the things that you want. I can't tell you what you want to do with your life; you need to find those answers for yourself to ultimately enable you to succeed long term. What I can say is, if you have a healthy body then you are more likely to be able to achieve whatever it is you want. Just losing weight is only the first step in that process.

How to Use the Warriors Programme

This is your manual for weight management. It is designed to be practical and hands-on. You can read this book from cover to cover, or you can dip in and out as you please, looking for more information on a particular subject, or to refresh your memory, once you are up and running with your plan.

However, when you do your Business Plan (in Chapter 5), you will not have enough information to hand, unless you have worked through the chapters on Nutrition (Chapter 3) and Exercise (Chapter 4) first. The key stages in the structure must be worked through in sequence. This is because you need to build your knowledge and understanding in order to move forward. These three stages are as follows:

1. Gather information, just as you would when setting up any new business. For your body/business you need to find out about nutrition and exercise to determine how to make it run successfully. (*Chapters 3 and 4.*)

2. Develop a unique Business Plan around your body, setting clear goals and objectives:
   - a clear definition of what you want from your body
   - an action plan – what you want, when you want it and how to achieve it
   - a selection of the best monitoring tools to measure progress (to save time you can also order a Warriors kit, which contains the necessary tools – see page 186)
   - set up a monitoring system, just as you would when running a business. (*Chapters 5 and 6.*)

3. Establish your personal levels of commitment and motivation to see the programme through. This will involve looking at why you want to change and how to create sufficient internal energy to ensure that you succeed. (*Chapter 7.*)

The additional factors

Having set the Warriors programme in motion, you need to consider the effects of your new attitude on the people around you. For that reason, Chapter 8 'Culture Change' will show you how to manage the expectations of your partner, family, friends and colleagues. Just as in a business, change involves people. In managing your body/business, you must take into consideration those around you, their needs and their aspirations, in order to gain their support and encouragement.

Time management is a vitally important factor in your life and it is dealt with in detail in Chapter 9, together with the implementation of your Business Plan. In order to succeed on the Warriors programme, you need to be able to find the right balance for work, exercise and focus. You do it automatically when running your business, and it is one of the transferable skills that you will be applying to your new body/business. This chapter also includes a practical guide to implementing the Business Plan you prepared in Chapter 5.

Your work probably brings with it a hectic lifestyle, and it is one that you cannot always predict. It involves a considerable amount of travel, staying in hotels and passing through airports, not to mention hours spent on the road. You may have little control over your food choice and intake, and limited opportunities for exercise. These aspects are covered in Chapter 10 'Handling External Pressures', where you will find tips and suggestions on how you can best cope in these circumstances.

Follow the Warriors programme and I assure you that **you will never have to go on another diet again**. You will lose weight *and*, more important still, find a way to keep it off. Above all, you will achieve your own standards and goals; ones set by you and no one else.

1
Going into Battle

Objectives

- To learn more about the Warriors programme and discover how it can be adapted to your individual requirements

- To find out why people become overweight

The Warriors programme is about weight and fitness management for the executive male. It uses the skills that you already possess in running a business to manage your body. I have called both the programme and the book 'Warriors', because managing your weight and fitness, like running a business, is akin to going into battle. You need the brains of a businessman and the spirit of a Warrior, so my company philosophy for Warriors is simple and unequivocal: 'Mentally strong – physically fit'.

All the key ingredients of good business management and strategy are here:

- The need to prepare
- The strength and energy that is used in learning new skills and then applying them
- The feeling of elation when things go right
- The sense of euphoria when a conquest is made.

You already have the skills of an executive. Now you will be applying those to the management of your body. You also possess the spirit of the Warrior. That spirit, that mind-set, that determination to succeed, the commitment to your word, that inner strength and resolve, will all be developed, to ensure your success – and to save your life.

How to Save Your Life!

I want you to know that if losing weight and keeping it off is your objective, then you will succeed. I wrote this book to help you get there. For, uniquely, the Warriors programme transforms the perceived problem – your body – into a company. How to run a company is an area you are extremely knowledgeable about, and by adopting this perspective you will be able to understand that you possess all the essential skills to manage your core business – your body/business. It also enables you to understand your needs and idiosyncrasies, and build a regime that is ideally suited to you, not some formula that is designed for a mass audience and has no relevance to *your* day-to-day life.

Have these questions come up for you recently?

- Do you want to be fit and healthy, with high energy and a great physique, but your reality is that of a busy executive with a stressful life, worried about your health?

- Have your doctor, partner or friends been suggesting that you should do something about your weight?

- Do you feel you have a lifestyle that makes any weight loss programme impossible?

If you answered yes to any of those questions, do not despair; this book is designed for you, based on my own experiences. And why am I so certain that the Warriors programme will work? Well, as you will have seen from the Introduction to this book, I too have suffered with a weight problem for most of my life, and from a very early age. I have tried innumerable diets, nearly all of which worked, but *none* lasted long enough to keep my weight managed over a long period. Why?

Diets didn't work for me because:

- They all involved me adapting to their requirements. So long as I slotted into their structure it worked. I could do that for a while, but not for a lifetime.

- None of them spoke my language. They were not designed for executives and they took no account of a busy, often high-pressure life, with little control over my food choices.

- As a male executive I felt that the weight management industry was very female oriented, with nowhere I could go for support and help with like-minded people. There seemed to be no one addressing the issues from a male standpoint, that is to say, more direct and focused, and more objective and goal oriented.

- None of them worked on what I see as the three key elements to weight management – mind-set, exercise and nutrition in one package, and at the same time. They concentrated, predominantly, either on nutrition, or exercise, and hardly touched the mind-set side at all.

By working on my own needs, I created a long-term plan for getting fitter, slimmer and mentally stronger, the 'ingredients' of which are common knowledge to you as a corporate executive. If you can run a business, you can run your body in the same way to produce the results you want. The 'business plan' you devise for your company is just as valid a tool to apply to your own growth and success. Just as you can take over a failing business and turn it around with careful planning, you can do the same with your body/business. I did it, and continue to help others achieve their own health and fitness goals. And if I can do it, so can you!

The Big Four Factors in Being Overweight

The first thing to do is think about why you are overweight. There are only four possible reasons for this – and these are the only factors I could find upon a thorough investigation.

- **Genetics** The one factor that is completely outside your control. There is nothing you can do to change this, but this book will give you strategies to counter its effects. Whatever your genetics, you can still decide to live a healthy life.

- **Nutrition** You are consuming too many calories from food and drink relative to the amount of energy you are using. You have to learn to befriend food so that it can still be enjoyable, but not do your health damage at the same time.

- **Exercise** You do not undertake enough exercise relative to the amount of food and drink you are consuming. Perhaps not as essential as nutrition to weight loss, but certainly essential for long-term weight management. Exercise is vital for the maintenance of a healthy body and it can have enormous benefits for your mental attitude and sense of well-being.

- **Mind-set** You may have an emotional attachment to food, which you will need to break. Food can become an abusive substance – rather like being an alcoholic. Mind-set issues also include stress, boredom and habit. To lose weight you must develop the will to change, together with the kind of attitude that will keep you focused when things get tough.

With these Big Four factors identified, I set about developing a strategy to counteract them. I realised that the battle had to involve all the disciplines of nutrition, exercise and mind-set in one coherent plan – uniquely, my programme combines these three key elements in one package.

And, if you have ever tried to lose weight before, you will know that the most difficult part is not getting the weight off in the first place, it's keeping it off. I designed the Warriors programme to focus on how to keep the weight off, so that all your efforts are not wasted after a few months, when all the weight is regained, with interest! As with any business, your aim should be long-term success.

I am certain that you will keep the weight off, once you have lost it, because:

- With the help and assistance of the Warriors programme, you will understand and apply a method of weight and fitness management that is unique to you and your needs

- You will transfer skills, which you already possess from your business experience, into the process of managing your body

- You will play to your strengths

- You will be so completely in control of your own weight management and fitness, that, as I promised in the Introduction to this book, you will **never need to follow another diet ever again**.

Key points

- With the Warriors programme your body becomes a core business; one that you manage along similar lines to your company

- To follow the programme you will concentrate on the three key pillars of weight management: mind-set, exercise and nutrition

- The programme is designed to ensure long-term success; not just a short-term 'fix' to get the weight off quickly

- The programme is built around you and plays to your personal strengths

2
Business Plan I – The Basics

Objective

- To discover how to apply the principles of a business plan to your weight management programme

Every business, from the largest corporation to the smallest one-man band needs a Business Plan. If you approach an investor to invest in your company, the first thing they will ask to see is your Business Plan, because they need to be assured that your business has a good chance of success, and they will want to see the steps you have planned on the way to that success. And, if they invest, they will wish to review your progress with you, following the steps of your plan.

In exactly the same way, your body/business needs a plan, but here the person you are trying to convince is you. Your body/business plan requires a solid structure, and cannot be just a series of half-hearted hopes.

The Business Plan Philosophy

Most businesses are about producing something, and your body/business is about enabling you to do the things you want to do with your life. I would hazard a guess that many of your aspirations cannot be achieved without having a body that is in condition to serve you in your cause. Certainly, having a body that is in the 'right' condition will help you enormously in your task. The business plan is something you, as an executive, can understand quite readily, as it applies to your body. As a method for helping you to see exactly how to manage your body and produce the results you want, it is something you will immediately see as relevant. For example, if your dream is simply driving down the stock levels (inventory) in your company, which is the equivalent of just losing weight, that will not enable your company to survive in the long-run. It will make your company more efficient – that is valuable and laudable. It will take you part of the way there, by freeing up valuable working capital (like having more energy in your body), but it won't achieve the objectives of the company because, ultimately, what the business needs is to produce, market and sell its product, not drive down stock levels. It may be a wonderfully efficient company, but what's it in business to do? What are you in business to do with your body/business – how can your body serve you in that process?

How Can a Business Plan Help You?

I believe that you *can* teach an old dog new tricks. I have lost 8 stones in weight, and re-educated myself about diet, nutrition and exercise. I am now running marathons and competing in triathlons at over 50, having started to do so as a complete novice in my late forties. I firmly believe, without false modesty, that I am not exceptional. The only exceptional part is that I'm an average person, who has managed to commit to a consistently long period of training and that has enabled me to participate in those sports – that is all. I am certain that everybody has the capacity to realise similar ambitions.

Running marathons and competing in triathlons may be far from your chosen dream, but if you are prepared to consistently work at it, taking tiny steps at a time, towards your goal, you will ultimately succeed. You can think of this as shifting grains of sand to move a mountain. While you are doing it each tiny grain seems to make so little difference, but do it consistently, over a sufficient period of time, and you will be astounded at the results. It is just what you already do in running your business. If you have a good Business Plan, with (SMART) (Sustainable, Measurable, Achievable, Realistic, Time-related) goals, where the stepping stones towards those goals are clear, and milestones are set, by when you wish to achieve those goals, then your chances of success are greatly enhanced – managing your body/business is no different.

You will find out how to prepare a Business Plan for your body/business in Chapter 5, but first you need to do a spot of information-gathering in the form of Chapters 3 and 4, where we look at the importance of understanding nutrition and the best way to exercise for your needs.

Key points:

- Every business, including your body/business, needs a Business Plan

- What is your dream for your body/business? What do you want your body to do for you?

- The plan for your body/business must contain SMART goals (or objectives)

- Before tackling the plan, it is important to gather information, just as you would if you took over a new department or acquired a new company

3
Business Input – Nutrition

Objectives

- To think about why you eat

- To discover what high-quality nutritional input is

- To use that knowledge to consume the right proportions and combinations of foods for your body's needs

- To learn how to monitor your eating and drinking

If you are well-armed with information about nutrition, you will understand how to get the best-quality intake to help you both lose weight and become healthier. Your knowledge will enable you to take control of how much you need to eat, what you can eat and how to monitor your eating (for an analysis of what you currently eat and how to build a personal food plan visit the Warriors website – see page 186).

Nutrition is a complex subject and a science in its own right, but in this chapter you will find the essential elements for your Warriors weight management programme. I have focused on the essence of what you need to achieve healthy weight loss and maintenance of your new weight, once you have achieved your target.

Before you actually undertake a weight-loss programme, however, it is essential that you write down your Picture in Words (see Chapter 6) first, to capture exactly how you feel *now*. Once you begin to lose weight, you will find it difficult to remember how it was for you at the outset, and those feelings of your readiness for change can be a vital driving force, when you need encouragement later on.

Eating for All the Wrong Reasons

Of course, the basic reason we eat and drink is to provide our bodies with fuel that is turned into energy to enable us to live. Food and drink have a very important social function too, and for many of us, they also become a coping mechanism.

Do you ever have the feeling, when you've just closed a fantastic deal, and you really want to celebrate, that the first thing you want to do is go out for a fabulous meal, with friends or family, and perhaps crack open a bottle of champagne? At the other end of the emotional scale, when you've had a bad day at the office, do you cheer yourself up with a glass of wine and a really 'good' meal?

Then there are those twin pillars of boredom and habit. How often do you go to fill up the car and buy something to eat on the way – just for something to do on the journey? Are there times when you get home, and out of sheer habit, head straight for the fridge? Or do you always have your first drink with some peanuts or a bag of crisps?

Perhaps there are other occasions like work-related drinks parties when the canapés are being handed round. You don't feel that hungry, but it's something to do with your hands – it's relaxing, just to take another mouthful of something. It helps to break up the conversations a bit. Is that habit, or stress – or perhaps a bit of both?

The Essentials of Nutrition

The two key factors that you must keep in mind at all times, when thinking about nutrition, are:

- **Nutrition** = Energy or Fuel (this is measured in calories – kcal)

- **Balanced Diet** = Nutrients from all the Food Groups

To follow the Warriors programme, you will need three very important items:

- a food diary
- a calorie counter
- a small kitchen scale.

All three are essential kit – why? Because you need to know how much energy (calories) you are putting into your body and you need to capture that data so that you have sufficient information for analysis of your progress (good or bad) later. (See Useful Addresses, page 186, for details of where to obtain all three items.)

The major platform of the Warriors programme rests on these simple principles:

- You are never, ever, going to be on a diet again.

- You will adopt a healthy eating programme of foods you like that fit in with your calorie requirements.

- You will eat less of those foods while losing weight and more when you are maintaining your new, reduced, weight.

Fuelling the Engine

Nutrition can be likened to the fuel for a factory, in this case your body/business. Good nutrition consists of taking in the correct quantities of protein, carbohydrates, fats and vitamins, the nutrients, to enable your body to function at its most productive and efficient.

To be more specific, it may be helpful to think of your body as a machine:

- **Carbohydrates** are the petrol going into the tank – that's your driving fuel.

- **Vitamins** are the spark plugs. You won't get combustion in the engine unless you have the spark plugs working properly – adequate amounts of vitamins are necessary, but not excessive amounts.

- **Fats** are the engine oil, and although fats get a bad press, we all need certain amounts of fat to function properly. Fats act as a lubricant for the skin and tissues, and also to help metabolise certain vitamins. But, if you eat too much, you're going to clog up the engine or, in the case of your body, it will be your arteries.

- **Protein** is absolutely essential, but the quantity that you eat is critical. Protein takes a long time to digest, and doesn't necessarily give you all the nutrients you require. High-protein diets may be fashionable, but they force your system through an enormous amount of work and create a lot of toxins in your body, which at a later stage you will have to eliminate, rather like an exhaust kicking out fumes. Yes, you will lose weight, but it's only in the short term, and what we are interested in for the Warriors programme is a safe way of eating that will sustain you, keep you healthy and with food that you enjoy. This way you will slowly but continuously lose weight through the programme, and maintain your preferred weight thereafter.

> There's no 'good' or 'bad' food; it's all good, it's all
> nutrition. It's the proportion and combination of food,
> that your body specifically needs, which is
> important.

What Your Body Needs

Are you ready to discover exactly what your body needs to be
fit, healthy and functioning optimally? Information is the key to
success here. More than fifty nutrients are needed by the body
daily, in various amounts, and a balanced diet with good variety will meet these requirements. When you reduce your food
intake it is even more important to follow healthy eating principles and taking nutritional supplements will not make up for
a poor diet. Although a one-a-day multivitamin/mineral, as an
'insurance policy', will do no harm, it may not be needed. To
follow our earlier example of the body being like a car: say your
car has six spark plugs. You get these six from a balanced diet,
but take an extra two as a supplement. These extra two spark
plugs will not make your car go any faster or make your body
any more efficient.

To find out what your body needs, you have to know which
foods go into which groups (including water and alcohol), and
how to find the right proportions of each food group in your
diet to suit your individual needs. Remember, water is vitally
important (drink at least 3½ pints (2 litres) per day), especially when losing weight, as it is one of the ways of eliminating the
toxins that will be thrown out by your body.

Calories and alcohol

I know that right now your diet may not look anything like ideal
– it may be totally unplanned and chaotic. But don't panic. By
following the advice here you will soon have things under control. You are not going to be asked to cut out alcohol and sugar
entirely, that is up to you. In fact some sugar is fine, provided

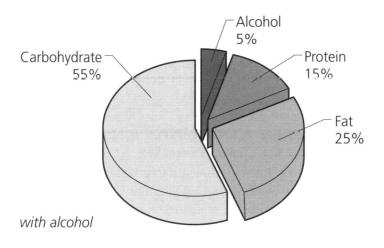

with alcohol

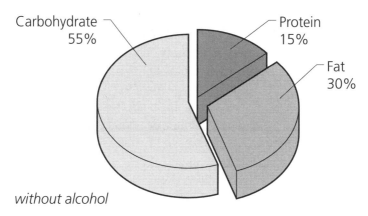

without alcohol

Alcohol makes a significant difference in your diet. The two pie charts show the recommended daily percentages of carbohydrate, fat and protein, with and without alcohol.

that the rest of the diet is balanced, and the key nutrients to target in any weight management programme are fat and alcohol.

At the start of a weight management programme, when you have most weight to lose, you will need to get the absolute best out of the calories you are consuming. Alcohol consists of relatively 'empty' calories, with low levels of nutrients, so it may be sensible to give it up for a while to maximise both your weight loss and the quality of your nutrition. A bonus of doing this is that you will feel much more energetic and much clearer-headed, and will suffer less from dehydration when you are exercising or travelling by plane.

The Energy Equation

Do you know what a calorie actually is? You will know that some foods are highly calorific and that you will need to reduce your intake, but what does this actually mean? Put simply, a calorie is the unit used to measure energy. On food labels you will see it listed as kcal or kjoule.

Weight maintenance equation:

- energy in   = energy out, plus or minus your fat stores

  or

- calories in = calories out plus or minus your calorie
  store (fat)

You can see from this that if you consume more calories than you need (or reduce the amount you exercise) you will put on weight and if you eat fewer calories than you need (or increase the amount you exercise) you will lose weight. Sounds simple, doesn't it? So there are three important questions for you to ask.

1. How much fuel do I need?
2. How do I apportion it correctly?
3. Which is more important, the calories you put in (eat and drink) or the calories you use up (physical activity)?

We will now look at each of these in turn.

1. How much fuel do I need?

Your daily requirements for energy can be calculated from your basal metabolic rate (BMR). This is the amount of energy you need every day to keep 'ticking over'. It is the energy that is needed by the important tissues of your body. Below is an approximation of how a 30–60-year-old, 13 stone (82.5kg) man burns kcal while resting in bed all day.

Organ	kcalories per day	% of metabolic rate
Brain	380	21%
Heart	180	10%
Kidney	125	7%
Liver	580	32%
Lung	165	9%
Other body tissues	380	21%

What is important about this is that your liver and brain need energy – approximately 50 per cent of your metabolic rate. Even when you are not active, sitting at a desk all day, your essential organs need fuel. Now you are certainly a lot more active than that, whatever your daily routine!

In order to help you to calculate your individual needs, follow the step-by-step guide below. But, bear in mind whatever your calorie intake is currently, that by cutting down by 500–600kcal a day you will produce the desired result of approximately 1 per cent loss of body weight per week. This is approximately equal to 1–2lb (0.5–1.0kg) a week, but it may not be that consistent. Some weeks will be more, and some less. When weight is lost sensibly, 75 per cent of that is fat and 25 per cent is muscle (protein) – this is the normal ratio. Exercise, particularly a programme of resistance exercise, may help to reduce the loss of muscle.

Here's how to work out your daily energy (kcalorie) requirements:

Step 1. Working out your basal metabolic rate – BMR (this is the total number of calories that you need to survive, when you do 'nothing').

You first need to record your weight in kilos

1 stone = 14lb   1lb = 0.45kg   My Weight____kg

Now, choose one of the equations below, and write in your weight in kg instead of the 'W' :

18–29 years   BMR = 15.1 x W + 692
30–59 years   BMR = 11.5 x W + 873
> 60 years   BMR = 11.7 x W + 585   My BMR____kcals

This figure gives you the minimum number of kcalories you need to keep essential organs functioning at your current weight (this will obviously change as you reduce weight). This figure represents the largest portion of your overall daily energy requirements. The additional amount of energy needed for everyday activities, work and exercise is usually much, much smaller than the BMR. This will vary considerably from person to person but, unless you are an élite athlete in training, it will not form a high percentage of your daily requirements.

Step 2. How to classify your occupation as light, moderate or moderate–heavy.

Obviously, how much energy you expend during your working day depends on what you do. For most managers and executives that would fall into the light category, unless your particular job involves a lot of walking around, but check this by using the following table:

Light	Moderate	Moderate–heavy
Administrative and managerial	Sales workers	Equipment operators
Professional and technical workers	Service workers	Labourers
Sales representatives	Domestic helpers	Agricultural, e.g. animal husbandry, forestry and fishing
Clerical and related workers	Students	
	Transport workers	
	Some construction workers, e.g. joiners, roofing workers	Some construction workers, e.g. bricklayers, masons

My Occupation Classification _____

Step 3. How to classify your non-occupation activity.

As well as working we all have other activities that take up energy. These include walking, gardening, washing the car and any sporting exercise such as swimming, squash, golf, or running. This is more difficult to classify as it depends upon a number of factors, including length of time actually engaged in the activity, your existing fitness level, your body composition and so on. Unless you are already taking part in a programme of regular physical activity, most people will fall into the non-active category. Be careful not to overestimate your exercise/non-occupation activity.

Non-active	Moderately active	Very active
Mostly drive with no additional exercise taken	Take part in vigorous exercise for 20 minutes at least 3–5 times a week	In active physical training at least once a day for 60 minutes or more per session
Occasional light activity carried out during the week		

My Non-occupation Classification_____

Step 4. Calculate your physical activity level (PAL).

Use the following table to give you an overall PAL figure of between 1.4–1.9:

Occupational Activity → ↓ Non-occupational activity	Light	Moderate	Moderate/Heavy
Non-active	1.4	1.6	1.7
Moderately active	1.5	1.7	1.8
Very active	1.6	1.8	1.9

My PAL = _____

Step 5. Your estimated energy requirements for your current weight.

Multiply your BMR by your PAL =
_____ kcals per day

Example: A 35-year-old manager weighs 15½ stone (100kg). He travels to work by train and uses his car the rest of the time. He has a 10-minute walk to and from the station each day, but other than this he takes no additional exercise outside his office life.

Weight	= 100kg
BMR = 11.5 x 100 + 873	= 2,023kcal each day
Occupational activity	= Light
Non-occupational activity	= Non-active
PAL	= 1.4
Total estimated daily kcal	= 2,023 x 1.4
	= 2,832kcal

It is very important that you understand the safe level at which you can lose weight. From your total estimated daily requirements for your current weight, subtract 500–600kcal a day. This will result in a safe weight loss of approximately 1 per cent or 1–2lb (0.5–1.0kg) each week. You may lose weight far more quickly in the first two weeks, but this should level off to a smaller and sustained weight loss. If weight is lost too fast you are losing more muscle than fat – this is undesirable. Go back and recalculate your requirements and double-check your food intake using your food diary (see below) and calorie counter (see Useful Addresses, page 186, for details of how to obtain one) to make sure that your maths are correct.

A 1 per cent loss of body weight may not seem very dramatic, but when weight is lost too fast (i.e. through cutting calories down too much), more muscle and lean tissue may be lost. Muscle is 'active' and requires more energy/calories to work, whereas fat requires far less energy. It is in your best interest to retain muscle and lose fat to maintain or improve body efficiency. Bottom line is that you can eat more without putting on weight if you have a body that has more muscle!

2. How do I apportion what I eat correctly?

The important things to look at are distribution, in terms of the **quantity of calories** consumed during the day and the **time of day** they are consumed. The 'mix' of food, where the calories come from, is the 'balance' in the diet.

Take a look at how you divide up your calories through the day. For example, it's a good idea to keep two of your three daily meals simple and concentrate on the one you spend some time either cooking or preparing. Breakfast could be carbohydrate from some form of cereal, such as porridge, taken with a piece of fruit and some coffee. Lunch can be quick and simple again – perhaps a sandwich and a piece of fruit. Evening could be when you have your largest meal, with the main piece of protein (fish, meat or perhaps pulses) in it. In percentage terms this could be:

25% on breakfast
30% on lunch
45% on dinner.

If you want to have snacks, or have your main meal in the middle of the day or some other time that is absolutely fine – just make life as simple as possible and try to set a routine that you can stick to and that suits your needs. If you want snacks mid-morning or afternoon that is fully acceptable too, but just remember to plan for them and count them into your daily calorie total.

The next question is how to get the right 'balance' of nutrients. Here is where I refer you to the 'food pyramid' which simply looks like this:

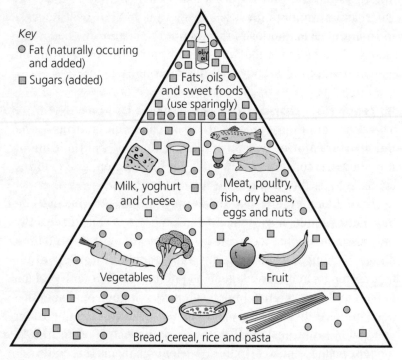

The food pyramid

Based on the food pyramid you can see that the main fuel comes from the 'bread, cereal, rice and pasta' group. You will notice that, as you go up the pyramid, you are getting less, to the point where you have relatively little 'fats, oils and sweets', which are shown at the apex. These are the ones that you want to consume least of all. Note, too, that there are also symbols of fats, oils and sugars throughout the pyramid showing that the other groups contain these nutrients. So remember that within each group you can make a lower or higher fat decision, such as full-cream milk versus semi-skimmed or skimmed milk. Note particularly that the pyramid shows the proportions in which to consume these varieties of foods. That really is important. To give you a clearer idea of the nutrients that go into each food group the table on pages 34 and 35 shows you the main ones.

The final thing to do is work out how to balance your calorie intake throughout the day so that you can feel you are eating reasonable portions and not going too hungry. Remember you may feel hungry or 'out of sorts', from time-to-time. This is a big change for your body. To lose weight it has to feed on itself. That will be uncomfortable, especially in the first few weeks, until you get used to your new food intake, so accept that there is a price to pay for a magnificent outcome.

3. Which is more important, the calories you put in (eat and drink) or the calories you use up (physical activity)?

The answer to this depends on what your main objective is. Exercise is beneficial for weight loss but essential for weight maintenance, whereas dietary management is essential for weight loss and important for weight maintenance. So, managing your calorie intake has a higher priority when trying to lose weight, but physical activity seems to be more important for weight maintenance. Physical activity will also aim to maintain or promote muscle growth, and that is beneficial on a weight-loss programme.

Goal Setting

In your Business Plan, which you will be working on in Chapter 5, you will establish what your SMART (Specific, Measurable,

Food groups for health and sport performance

	Bread, cereals and potatoes	Fruit and vegetables
Good examples	Wholemeal bread, white bread, bagels, porridge, cornflakes, jacket potatoes, currant buns, scones, malt loaf, rice, plain biscuits, noodles, low-fat chips	Bananas, apples, oranges, canned tomatoes, sweetcorn, peas, mushrooms, onions, raisins, sultanas, fruit juice
Sports performance functions	Ideal fuel for hard exercise	Many functions including fighting infection, help repair, nutrients in fruit and vegetables convert food into energy
Main nutrients	Carbohydrate (for energy) B vitamins Some calcium (white flour and bread and some breakfast cereals) Iron Protein	Vitamin C Betacarotene Folates Carbohydrate (especially in fruit Fibre
How much to eat	Lots	Lots
Tasty tips	• Go for wholegrain cereals • Go easy on the spread on bread and potatoes • Watch the creamy pasta sauces	• 'Pump out' sand-wiches with salad vegetables • Don't add fat or rich sauces to vegetables

Milk and milk products	Meat, fish and alternatives	Fatty and sugary foods
Milk, cheese, fromage frais, yoghurt, milk-shakes and yoghurt drinks (does not include eggs, butter, mayonnaise, cream)	Beef, minced beef, lamb, pork, chicken, turkey, sardines, tuna pilchards, cod, baked beans, kidney beans, chick peas, seeds, e.g. sunflower, nuts, eggs	Chocolate*, butter, mayonnaise, low-fat spreads, margarine, cooking oils, cream, crisps, cream-filled and fancy biscuits, sweets, sugar, honey, jam*
Strong bones, nails and teeth	Prevent anaemia Tissue growth and repair	Some sugar and sugary foods (*)can be a fuel source for high-energy sports and for use at competitions
Calcium Protein Vitamin B12 Vitamins A and D	Iron Protein B vitamins, especially B12 Zinc Magnesium	Some vitamins and minerals (e.g. vitamin E in olive oil), but also a lot of fat and/or sugar and salt
Moderate amounts	Moderate amounts and choose lower-fat varieties	Use wisely during training and competition as part of your high-carbohydrate diet
• Choose lower-fat varieties, e.g. semi-skimmed milk • Grate cheese to make it go further • Compare food labels and watch that fat!	• Use more vegeta-bles and less meat in cooking • Remove skins and trim visible fat • Beans are rich in carbs – eat 'em up!	• More bread may mean more spread – scrape it on • Watching your weight? Go easy on this group

Achievable, Realistic, Time-related) objectives are going to be. If any of those are related specifically to targeted weight loss then there are a couple of points to explore further.

What do you think is a 'healthy' weight for you and how did you arrive at that figure? Is it based on your own ideas, media images, family pressures or just what you think you 'ought' to look like?

You need to get rid of the idea of an 'ideal' weight except in the sense of it being ideally suited to you and your circumstances. There is an abundance of ways to measure your 'ideal' standard. The classic one is the scales – the weight measure. There is also body mass index (BMI) and even simple waist measurement. All have their followers and their logical arguments. Whatever measure you decide on, make sure you are comfortable with it – that you believe it is the right one for you. Discuss the alternatives with your GP and your fitness trainer, and agree which measure you wish to set as your standard. There is no right or wrong one – it is what you feel suits your needs best. Do not get too hung up about it, it's only one measure – what really matters is how you feel and what you want your body to be able to do for you.

In terms of nutritional goals, what you're trying to do is, first of all, to find out what you need to eat in terms of quantity, relative to what you want to lose. The nutrition side is essentially about weight management or weight loss and you're trying to measure how many calories you need to get a healthy and safe long-term weight loss. Your goals are around finding an eating pattern, a food combination that not only suits you but you can maintain for the rest of your life. This is not just for a limited period, or for a short-term reduction of weight. You must be absolutely clear that you are now going to choose combinations of foods that will be exactly the same whether you're going for weight loss, or maintaining your weight. The only difference between these two modes – weight loss and maintenance – is that the amount of calories (the quantity you consume) will vary up and down depending on what your objective is.

Translating Calories into Food and Drink

Now you need to start thinking about how many calories your food and drink contains and what sort of choices you are going to have to make. Calorie counting is usually thought of in terms of unpalatable foods, composed or consisting of ingredients that you do not like and would not choose to eat. Indeed, the whole idea of counting calories and recording them is boring, to say the least, and most of us also firmly believe that dieting makes you hungry and miserable. Well, it doesn't have to be like that.

> The first rule of a successful weight management routine is 'Do what you enjoy, not what you feel you have to.'

Let's assume that you are having a daily calorie intake equal to 2,200kcal. There are lots of ways you can achieve that. Here are some examples:

- **A typical business lunch or reception** with sausage rolls, vol-au-vents, quiche, dips and alcohol

- **A fashionable quick-fix diet,** which includes excessive amounts of only one item throughout the day, say fruit and vegetables, or just protein

- **A balanced day** with a wide variety of foods (meat, fish, pasta, rice, fruit and vegetables). If the chosen items are fat-reduced, then a high volume of food is achievable

- **An extreme option** where all the calories come from only chocolate or alcohol or just one 'blow-out' meal

Obviously not all these options are healthy and only one will help you achieve sustainable long-term weight management. A 'balanced' day for most effective weight loss includes lots of fruit and vegetables, plenty of starchy carbohydrates, some protein, and some milk and dairy foods. You can also include some foods higher in sugar, depending on what your overall calorie need is, and whether you are involved in a lot of exercise. If your exercise level is low then you would want to keep higher sugar foods to a minimum. Research has shown that it is more difficult to gain weight on a high carbohydrate diet compared with one high in fat, but *all calories do count*. What you are looking at, overall, is to reduce the total calorie intake – that is what takes priority when managing your weight and certainly you are looking to keep to a minimum all foods that are high in fat and alcohol.

Fat facts

Remember, if you consistently eat and drink more kcalories than you actually need, you will put on weight, or will fail to lose weight.

However, weight for weight, some nutrients provide more kcalories than others. For instance, 1g of fat provides 9kcal, 1g of alcohol provides 7kcal, 1g of carbohydrate provides 4kcal and 1g of protein also provides 4kcal. This illustrates clearly how reducing your fat and alcohol intakes will have the greatest impact on your efforts to manage your weight sensibly. Nutrition scientists have found that high-fat foods do not make you feel so full that you stop eating. The result of this is that you continue to eat beyond the point of satisfying hunger, in other words, you overeat. High protein and high carbohydrate foods are much less likely to cause over-consumption.

A large intake of fat also does long-term damage because you consume a huge amount of calories with a relatively small amount of food. You are paying a really high price for a very small amount of nutrition. If you have ever said, 'I hardly eat anything, yet I still can't lose weight', think about exactly what you are eating.

As we have already seen, though, a weight management programme should never be 'fat free' or extremely low in fat, since a small amount of fat is essential for optimum health. Your body needs essential fatty acids and the fat-soluble vitamins (A, D, E and K). If your diet is too low in fat (less than 20 per cent of your daily energy needs), it becomes extremely difficult for the body to get everything it requires.

A note on fats

Although some oils and fats are high in unsaturated fats, such as the monounsaturated fat found in olive oil and polyunsaturated fat found in sunflower oil, they still contain the same amount of calories as saturated animal fats. Overall, it is important to moderate all types. As a guiding principle, keep your 'obvious' fat intake low. Cut down on things like cheese, cream and full-fat milk and go for skimmed milk instead or perhaps semi-skimmed as a compromise. Poultry stores a lot of its fat in the skin so remove it before cooking. Accept that however hard you try, fat will get into your diet anyway, through foods like lean meat, bread and cereals, which all contain small amounts.

If you have a particular medical reason for paying attention to your fat intake, consider consulting a dietitian (visit the Warriors website, details page 186) about your needs.

Looking at Labels

Once you start thinking in terms of nutritionally valuable food, you need to know how to assess what you are getting. A calorie counter will help with that, but you could also start looking

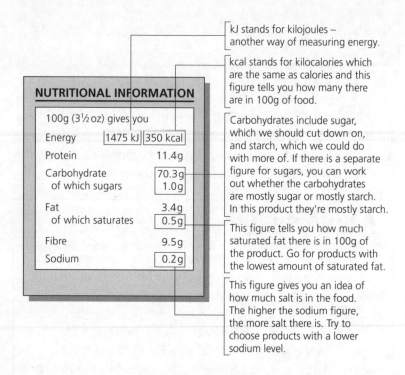

A typical food label

at the label content of the things you buy. Nutritional information is typically presented as per 100g of food and often per portion. However, bear in mind that what the label states as a portion may differ from your typical portion size. For fresh food you need a good set of food weighing scales to really calculate accurately.

Some 'Rules' of Weight Management

As with any other business, the cardinal rule when managing your weight is to pay close attention to planning. It is critical – a failure to plan is planning to fail. Knowing the rules of weight loss will help you plan effectively. The four most important rules are as follows:

- set targets
- assume a small, gradual rate of weight loss
- plan your meals
- self-monitor and evaluate.

Getting Practical

Based on your knowledge, so far, draw up your own suggested eating plan for a sample day. You could photocopy this table and use it later as a base for drawing up a healthy eating plan for yourself for next week. If you have the Warriors Kit (see Useful Addresses, page 186), use the Food and Mood Diary now or get a notebook, which will become your Food and Mood Diary, designated for the purpose of recording your intake and mood response.

Date and Time	Planned Food/Meal	Calories: Weight and Quantity	Actual	Mood and Response
		Total:		

Your Food and Mood Diary is a vital part of the information-gathering process for your body/business – indeed it is the bookkeeping department of the company. In it you will record everything that you eat and drink. There are four key elements to this important document:

1. Record what you **intend and plan** to eat – ideally for one week ahead.

2. Record any deviations from your planned food intake.

3. Record your reasons for and any emotional response you had when deviation from your plan occurred.

4. Review your reasons for deviating from your planned intake at regular intervals, say weekly for a quick review and monthly for a more in-depth analysis. This is to see if any patterns have emerged.

It may seem like a desperately boring task to note down and measure all your food intake, certainly at the outset and until you get more practised at it. But, when running your business, stock control is crucial: if you had suppliers rolling up with deliveries, you wouldn't just open up the gates and take them in without counting and checking the orders. It's the same with your body/business. You have to plan ahead and then count what has come in (food intake), and what goes out (your weight), so you have accurate stock levels. And, once you get used to it, you will find it keeps you extremely focused and it gives you a clear understanding of what you are doing.

From these figures you could also plot your weight on a graph, and plot your calorie intake alongside – it is interesting to see the co-relationship between the two, over a period of time. It's a bit like looking at the energy or fuel supply to your company, when you are also trying to reduce the amount of fuel you already have in stock.

The final Mood and Response column of your Food and Mood Diary is in some ways the most important, as it shows your response to specific foods and your emotional state around eating. Food, drink and everyday situations can all be potential triggers that can lead you into uncontrolled eating. This section of the diary is where you can identify them and analyse patterns.

Here's a typical example of part of a day's food and mood diary:

13 September

Time	Planned food/meal	Calories i.e. weight and quantity	Actual	Mood and response
7a.m.	Porridge 50g Milk 200 ml	180 68	Plus coffee	Buzz from coffee
10a.m.	1 apple, small	60		
1p.m.	Pitta bread/ salad with ham	350	Plus glass of wine – extra 200 cals	Headache, guilty about wine
3p.m.	Cup of tea	10	Plus biscuits – extra 55 cals	Angry with myself about wine and a bit hungry

If you really don't want to count calories or keep a food diary, you don't have to, but to have any chance of long-term success you must:

- know how much energy you are consuming
- know how the energy consumed relates to what you want to do with your weight, i.e. lose it or remain the same.

How you do that is up to you, but most successful long-term weight managers have found that knowing the amount of calories consumed and recording them against planned consumption is the best method.

Establishing a Routine

You may find that planning on a weekly basis is very difficult because you don't know exactly what your week is going to turn out like. Well, that's fine, it's just like running a company. You don't know whether suddenly the lights are going to go off in the factory or a machine is going to break down, so you're always dealing with unexpected events as they happen.

Of course, in previous generations, the week's menus were carefully planned and adhered to. For example, the Sunday roast lamb was followed by the leftovers in shepherd's pie on Monday. Food was bought with a weekly plan in mind. Today, however, there is a huge freedom of choice, but if you make an eating plan and stick with it, temptation is less likely to worry you.

It will also help because you do not have to think about what you were going to eat at the time when you were hungriest – just before a meal. You feel hungry, your appetite is sharp and you're thinking about what you can have to eat. Plan ahead and avoid all the pitfalls – know exactly what you intend to eat, ahead of time!

Where Are Your Weaknesses?

It helps your planning if you know where your weak areas lie. Perhaps, like me, you really need to feel full, particularly at night, and that means a lot of food. It was quantity, huge portions, which were a real issue for me. Or do you crave fat–protein combinations like sausages, hamburgers, salamis and cheeses?

Unless your diet is satisfying you won't be able to convert it into a lifetime habit of healthy eating. That is why conventional diets often fail. You have to try and find a way to steer a middle course between the sort of quantities and the combination of foods that you want, but at the same time not living on traditional diet food, such as salads, or fashionable diets that are based on one ingredient such as fruit, protein or vegetables. You have to find, or invent, recipes that fool your palate as they taste good, but are also positively supporting your weight loss by being low in calories at the same time. (For recipe ideas see the cookbooks in the Further Reading, page 195.)

A quick reminder

Quantity:

Do you know how many calories your body needs per day, to maintain your present weight? (Amount____)

Do you know how many calories you need from now on for a healthy weight loss (500–600 per day less than the above amount)? (Amount____)

Do you have a calorie-counting book?

Do you have kitchen scales to measure quantities?

Distribution:

Do you know how you will distribute your calories each day, e.g. 25% at breakfast, 30% at lunch and 45% for the evening meal? Or, are you going to plan in some snacks? If so, when and how many? (Note down the percentages for an ordinary day: Breakfast____% Lunch____% Dinner____% Snacks____% Alcohol____%)

Do you know how to balance the proportions in the food groups?

Monitoring:

Do you have a Food and Mood Diary ready for use and do you know how to use it?

Have you got a system of plotting your weight, e.g. on graph paper or on a computer?

Are you ready and able to plan your meals for the week ahead? (Have you done so? If not, start now.)

Location:

Have you selected certain locations where you will or will not eat? (It's helpful to ensure that you eat when it's appropriate to you, i.e. if you decide you will not eat at your desk or in the office, or in front of the television, then that is one way to cut down on snacks.)

Have you thought about who supplies you with your food and whether they need to be aware of what you now want to achieve? Do they understand what is needed? (This is information that you will use in the Business Plan in Chapter 5.)

Key points

- Think SMART (specific, measurable, achievable, realistic and time-related) when setting goals.

- Self-monitor with a food diary.

- Use a good calorie counter.

- Use food scales to monitor your calorie count accurately.

- Read food labels.

- Weigh yourself once or twice a week on the same set of scales at the same time of day.

- Plot your weight changes, ideally on graph paper or on a computer. This can be used in conjunction with your calorie records to show your weight loss history over a period of time.

- Recalculate your BMR and PAL at regular intervals – say once a month.

- Review your calorie requirements at times of weight plateaux, weight gain, excessive weight loss or after 11lb (5kg) weight loss.

- Maintain a 500–600kcal deficit per day for weight loss.

- Don't lose more than 1 per cent of your body weight in a week.

- Distribute your calories through the day in the way you wish to consume them. You may wish to stick to three set meals per day or you may wish to build in some snacks – just know, ahead of time, what you plan to do. This is important so that you can gradually build up a picture of where food consumption may have something to do with other aspects of your life – not just nutrition (fuel), which is its essential purpose.

- Do not crash-diet. Drastic calorie reduction can affect mental and physical performance, cause depression and promote obsession with food and eating.

- Aim for a balanced diet with plenty of variety.

- Enlist the help of others to help build and evaluate your plan of action.

- Realise that the programme is about a style of eating for life, not a quick-fix weight loss.

- For further help and advice on nutrition, including a service that will analyse your diet, look at the Warriors website (see Useful Addresses, page 186).

4
Exercise

Objectives

- To establish one of the best policies of your business

- To decide what goals you want to achieve from exercise

- To find out your current fitness and wellness status

- To decide the 'how, when, where and what' of your exercise programme

In the 'holy trinity' of weight management, exercise is one of the key players. Mind-set and nutrition are vital components of the Warriors programme, but without adding in exercise you won't be able to get the maximum long-term benefit in terms of weight loss, fitness and a positive mental attitude about yourself and your body.

Warning: Though you may be tempted to embark straight away on an exercise programme, don't take any action until you have completed Chapter 6 of this book, 'A Picture in Words'. Remember, this chapter is designed to arm you with information to help in the preparation of your Business Plan.

Think of your body as being like a car that you have left in the garage for a couple of months while you are away on business.

During that time it has not been used. When you come back, it's likely that the battery's run down and the oil will have stuck in the sump. You know that when you want to get the car going again it will need a service before you can get it out on the open road. Your body is just the same. If you stop using it, then you will gradually lose suppleness, strength and energy. How much you want to use it, however, is, to a large extent, up to you.

What Shape is Your Body/Business In?

When you take over a business, or are planning any major changes to the structure of a company, you need to know exactly what shape it is in. Start here and think about what you need to know about your body/business before going any further:

- Find out your fitness level *(think: when and where)*

- Have an overall health check *(think: how/with whom)*

- Assess where the company/your body is now *(think: any health-related problems/joints/weaknesses)*

- Set some benchmarks, standards that you want to operate at *(think: level of fitness/frequency of training/strength or endurance)*

- Set goals and objectives, make them short, realistic and achievable *(think: some event that you want to take part in/some physical activity you have wanted to do for a long time and cannot right now)*

- What are your outcome goals? *(think: what do you want your body to do for you)*

- What end result is it you want to achieve? *(think: what's your dream?)*

- What time and effort are you willing to make? (*think: how much time do you have? What real commitment are you prepared to make?*)

The Importance of a Physical Check-up

Wellness is about informed, educated choices. It is, therefore, important and sensible always to see your doctor for a check-up before doing any increased physical activity. While exercising you are putting yourself at a temporarily increased risk of having a heart attack or other cardiac incident. The people most at risk tend to be those who were active sports people in their youth, have had ten or more years of sedentary living, and go back in as though they are still young and fit. You are about to embark on a lifetime of improved living and a healthier existence, so taking some time to prepare properly and doing a feasibility study is time well spent. The benefits from the increased activity far outweigh the risks you expose yourself to when exercising. Seek the advice of experts, listen to your body and change things gradually and you minimise any minor risks.

Getting Started

When you have had a physical check-up, decided what you want to achieve and set some benchmarks then – paradoxically – it's time to stop and ensure that you are being realistic. When I started out, it was difficult for me to walk more than 55 yards (50m). My ankles and my feet hurt and my lower back ached, but I gradually built up from that level. Eventually, I managed to run a marathon, but I certainly couldn't do it overnight. Anybody who runs a marathon knows that it takes at least six months' training, even when you're in reasonably good condition at the outset. Even if your present targets are more modest, you still need to begin the process of thinking about the habitual activity plan you will design for yourself that will work **with your life**. The key here is to allow yourself a sense of achievement over short periods. So, if you want to run a marathon within two years of starting the Warriors programme, you would begin by setting a realistic target like being able, within a couple of weeks, to walk a mile or two without being breathless or in pain.

You cannot expect your body/business to achieve miracles overnight. It takes time to turn an inactive, perhaps mothballed company, around. Get it on the right track first, and stay with it. That will ensure that it becomes a long-term venture, one that has a long and healthy future. You're not going for just the quick fix any longer.

Why Bother with Exercise?

If you haven't thought about exercise since you were at school, you may not see the point in it. Surely having a good attitude to food and diet is enough? Well, no it isn't. Exercise is essential: if you don't use your body, and particularly if you don't use your muscles, they will atrophy. You need to keep yourself supple and moving if you want to enjoy longer and older age.

It's an extraordinary thing, but it doesn't really matter what age you are or where you are on the scale or what particular starting point you have, you will always be able to benefit from exercise. For example, a study in the US on very much older people showed that the regeneration of muscle can be quite phenomenal. People who were virtually bedridden could actually get up and enjoy a reasonable walk of a couple of miles all within a space of a few months. There is a great deal of evidence, both anecdotal and scientific, to support the view that increasing your levels of physical activity will increase energy levels, improve sleep quality, make you more productive, and enable you to manage stress more successfully.

There are also other, more obvious health benefits to regular exercise, including a reduced risk of premature heart disease, stroke and some cancers. Many people find that they are more able to keep up with their children, get around better as they become older, enjoy their skiing holidays more and recover faster from minor illnesses. Is that something that you also desire and aspire to?

The Wellness Continuum

We all have a perception of how healthy we are. The Wellness Continuum, illustrated opposite, shows a line upon which we all exist, somewhere along the continuum. We all start out at a neutral point and can move in either direction according to the lifestyle we choose.

The general path of many of us today is towards the Illness end of the continuum. We all expose ourselves to risks and gradually our bodies adapt to that slothful and unthinking existence. There is good news though, because no matter where you are on the continuum you can reverse any trend that you have started. By becoming aware of positive behaviours, adopting them, obtaining reinforcement and developing a positive attitude towards your ability to control your life, you can become much fitter and more healthy.

Wellness can be seen as a behaviour rather than a result. It is a journey towards mastery as you define it. No one else can tell you what Wellness means to you. You can get advice, seek assistance and listen to expert opinion, but you are the one who defines Wellness for you.

You can enjoy your body far more if you do take exercise, but you don't have to go to extremes. Your aim is to train and develop your body into the condition that you want it to be, for the things that you want to do. This means looking at the outcomes you hope to achieve from increasing your physical activity and enhancing wellness. Most fitness programmes only look at the outcomes you wish to achieve, but running alongside that is another very important factor. That is to make the process as rewarding, enjoyable and focused an experience as possible. It is not always realistic for exercise itself to be fun. But by setting out in the right way, with the right attitude and with the right goals, you at least give yourself a good chance of enjoying the experience through making real progress and seeing a gradual improvement in your physical condition.

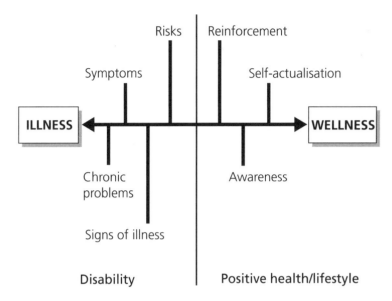

The Wellness Continuum

What are your outcome goals?

- Weight loss?
- Improved muscle tone?
- Stress control?
- Increased energy?
- General fitness?
- To play sports?
- To prevent illness?
- To slow down deterioration?
- To keep up with the children (or grandchildren)?
- What is the outcome you most want to achieve?

What time and effort are you willing to give to the achievement of these goals? What landmark goals can you set yourself? Think about these things, and develop your own thoughts, as you continue to read through this chapter. If you can be clear about what you want to achieve, right from the outset, this will help you when the going gets tough (as it inevitably will). Your conclusions will also help you as you come to develop your Business Plan in Chapter 5.

Planning Your Exercise Programme

What is your average day? I am not suggesting you change your whole working life, but take time to think about these questions:

- Do you walk, take the lift, catch a bus, go by car?
- Why don't you currently exercise?
- When do you have uninterrupted time to exercise?
- Where are you going to exercise?
- What exercise will you do?
- How often can you exercise?
- Who can support or help you with your programme?

From those questions you will have some realistic answers about what you can currently do, so let's look in more detail about how you will benefit from an exercise routine. Even the most modest amount of exercise has enormous benefit, but you need to know exactly what is the specific gain you are going to get. What do you want as well as weight loss? Below are just some of the benefits exercise can bring, but you need to think about what you would add to this list that would make you start, and keep on, exercising:

- increased energy
- improved sleep
- greater productivity
- better ability to cope with stress
- improved sex drive and performance
- reduced anxiety and depression
- more positive outlook
- weight loss

- improved muscle tone
- ability to participate better in social activities.

When to Exercise

We will look at what kind of exercise to do later, but now it's time to think about finding the time in your everyday life to exercise. What time of day is best for you? Consider two things. First, when do you feel at your most energetic and therefore most likely to have the get-up-and-go to exercise? Second, when are you least likely to get interrupted and find an excuse to stop? Balance these two factors out and decide when you think is going to work best for you.

If possible, early mornings can be ideal for three reasons. You are very unlikely to be interrupted, it cuts out the need for showering twice in the day and you won't feel the sword of Damocles hanging over your head all day. You can hop out of bed, do a nice gentle warm-up activity (more of what to do later) and gradually build yourself up to an effort level where you'll get slightly breathless. When you're finished, step into the shower, feeling refreshed, eat a good breakfast and you're ready for the challenges of the day.

To sum up, ask yourself:

- What time of day is best for you? Are you a morning or evening person?

- What best fits your 'normal' routine?

- When in a standard week could you confidently schedule some activity into your programme?

- Can you jog to the office, walk up the stairs, have a lunchtime swim?

- How can you plan for unusual circumstances?

- Will a business trip disrupt your routine?

Finding time in your usual routine is not usually a problem; it's the unusual circumstances that can throw you off course. When you are travelling away, unusually busy, approaching year end, negotiating a big contract, producing a big report (i.e. most weeks!), how are you going to plan to succeed in looking after your health? Exactly where does exercise fit into your list of priorities?

And don't imagine that exercise is just about the particular routine you have decided on. You're always going to be looking for the opportunity to do some more, like climbing the stairs, parking the car further away from the office or getting off one stop earlier from the bus. Soon you are going to start to become opportunistic about exercise and grab any chance that comes your way.

How Long will Your Exercise Programme Take?

Once you have answered the questions about when you are going to exercise, you need to start thinking sensibly about the actual time it will take. If you want to keep a reasonably healthy body – particularly in terms of aerobic exercise – then theoretically you should probably do three to five sessions a week of a minimum of half an hour each. My philosophy doesn't include setting hard-and-fast rules, but to start with three sessions a week is about right.

> When you're busy and stressed, the best way to clear your head and freshen up is to do a swift 15 to 20 minute bout of activity, take a shower and return to your work. Forty minutes away from your desk and you'll feel like you've taken half a day off!

Where to Exercise

Once you have decided on the time you have available to exercise, you need to actually plan where and when you are going to exercise within your week. Whatever your intended form of exercise is, it needs to be fitted into your overall time management system. Once you have done that, it is easier to adjust the plan to suit your schedule on a daily basis.

There are plenty of options available for you to consider – at home, work and outside resources. At home you can use keep-fit and training videos, weights, exercise machines and outside the house you can go jogging and walking. When away on business you can pack something light like a Dynaband, or your jogging shoes and make sure you stay in a hotel with a gym or swimming pool. Outside resources include gyms and swimming pools, cardiovascular classes, or sports facilities such as golf or athletic clubs and personal trainers.

What Exercise to Do

Here's where a bit more science gets involved. Often this is the point at which the advice of an experienced personal trainer or fitness instructor will be useful. However, with a little bit of careful consideration and a sensible approach you can design an appropriate activity programme for yourself.

The first thing to consider here is your metabolism. You should be thinking about speeding up your metabolic rate whenever you get the opportunity – not just through exercise.

Tips for increasing your metabolic rate

- do not sit still if you can fidget

- do not sit down when you can stand up

- do not stand still when you can walk

- do not walk slowly when you can move briskly.

The basic premise for this is quite straightforward. The more habitual you can make your activity, the more you can incorporate some consistent behaviours that embed themselves into your lifestyle, the more chance you have of long-term success. Your body will be consistently using more energy than it used to and therefore creating increased output on the profit-and-loss account of your body/business.

Let's Get FITT

Now we need to get a little more technical and have a look at the FITT principles – Frequency, Intensity, Time and Type of activity:

- Frequency: 'How often should I exercise?'
- Intensity: 'How hard should I work?'
- Time: 'How long should I exercise in each session?'
- Type: 'What type of exercise is best? Sports or exercise?'

Frequency: 'How often should I exercise?'

The Activity Continuum chart opposite is a useful guide to how to approach your progress. All movement along the continuum should be gradual. If you are doing nothing right now, then try to incorporate a small amount of activity into your schedule for the next few weeks. Then take a review of what you have learned, successes and failures, and then try to do a bit more. Only move up a level when you are confident and comfortable that your body and your lifestyle are adapted to the new levels. Rushing this progress is a guaranteed way to set yourself up to relapse to doing absolutely nothing again. If your eventual goal is to complete a marathon or some other intense activity, then eventually you should aim to progress towards the extreme end of the continuum. So where are you now?

I recommend that you try to build up to a consistent level of activity. If you are a creature of consistent habit and every day

Nothing	1x20 minutes per week	3x20 minutes per week	3x60 minutes per week	5x60 minutes per week
Start point for most people	Enough to reap some health benefits	Start to improve fitness levels significantly	Large improvement in fitness levels will be seen	Beyond this you risk injury and illness

Illness → Health → Fitness → Optimum Wellness

The Activity Continuum

suits you better than three times a week, then vary your activity and keep it to 30 to 45 minutes per day. Even at this level you will undoubtedly encounter feelings of burn-out and fatigue at times. These are danger times when you can very easily become tired, run down and disillusioned with your progress. Activity can then become a chore rather than an invigorating pleasure.

Warning: Available research tells us that more than five bouts of one hour of activity per week does seem to put you at more risk of injury and illness. Unless you are training for sporting activity there is very little you can gain as the risks seem to outweigh the benefits once this amount is exceeded.

To sum up, the ideal **frequency** to strive for is to plan every other day with some programmed physical exercise and then incorporate more habitual activity – like walking up stairs – into your daily life on an ongoing basis. So, even on your non-programmed days you are still affecting your energy account in a positive way.

Intensity: 'How hard should I work?'

It is vital to bear in mind how hard you should be working to ensure your safety while exercising. The essential balance to strike is between safety and achievement. At all times, if in doubt, err on the side of caution.

There are many ways of measuring your intensity levels during activity. All have their relative strengths and weaknesses. The best way to start is with a marriage between objective measurements and subjective feelings. It's a process of education to identify how your body feels at different levels of effort and intensity. And it's not just the physical symptoms you need to consider, like aching muscles or shortness of breath, but how you are feeling mentally. At what point are you ready to give up; if you keep going a little longer do you start to feel better, energised, confident? Understanding this relationship between body and mind will enable you to be in a position to monitor yourself easily, and achieve a far higher degree of success.

Taking your heart's measure

The best recommended objective measure is heart rate. To check this, the most accurate means is to buy a monitor with chest strap and wrist receiver. These are available from most good sports stores and certainly from specialist running shops (or see Useful Addresses, page 191). A heart-rate monitor will give you accurate physiological feedback on what is going on in your body.

The easiest way to take a look at the right intensity level is to use a guideline relative to your age. Your maximum heart rate will be roughly 220 beats per minute (bpm) minus your age. So a 50-year-old man will have a maximum heart rate of about 170bpm while a 30-year-old man has a maximum heart rate of approximately 190bpm.

Note it down now. *My maximum heart rate is* (220 – My Age) = _____(a)

> **Warning:** If ever you get anywhere near your maximum heart rate you are working too hard or to excess!

Of course, knowing your maximum heart rate is not enough to provide you with the information you need to find a safe, effective range in which to exercise. The next step is to find out your resting heart rate. The best time to measure this is when you first thing in the morning after naturally waking up from a restful night's sleep. An average resting heart rate is between 50 and 90bpm. Your resting heart rate will tend to lower as you get fitter. There are many factors that can affect your resting heart rate, so it's a good idea to take these measures over a number of days and use the lowest figure recorded.

Note it down. *My resting heart rate is* _____ (*b*)

Taking our 50-year-old example, with a maximum heart rate of 170bpm (a), let's say their resting heart rate is 75bpm (b). Calculate the difference between their maximum and resting heart rate by subtracting (b) from (a). This is called the heart rate reserve and in this example is 170 – 75 = 95bpm (c).

Maximum Heart Rate (a) _____ – Resting Heart Rate (b) _____ = _____ (c)

Note yours down now. *My heart rate reserve is*_____*(c)*

Now you need to consider different percentages of your heart rate reserve.

Your figures	Example (50-year-old)
50% of (c) = ... bpm (d)	50% of 95 = 47bpm
60% of (c) = ... bpm (e)	60% of 95 = 57bpm
70% of (c) = ... bpm (f)	70% of 95 = 66bpm
80% of (c) = ... bpm (g)	80% of 95 = 76bpm
90% of (c) = ... bpm (h)	90% of 95 = 85bpm

To give you your working zone you now need to add this percentage of heart rate reserve on to your resting heart rate.

Your figures	Example (50-year-old)
50% (d) + (b) = … bpm	47 + 70 = 117bpm
60% (e) + (b) = … bpm	57 + 70 = 127bpm
70% (f) + (b) = … bpm	66 + 70 = 136bpm
80% (g) + (b) = … bpm	76 + 70 = 146bpm
90% (h) + (b) = … bpm	85 + 70 = 155bpm

When you first start exercising, try to achieve around a rate of 50–60 per cent of your heart rate reserve. As you get fitter, you may be able to increase this gradually towards 70–80 per cent. As always, steady progress and gradual change are the keys to success.

Observing the signs

Along with monitoring your heart rate, you should also pay attention to how your body *feels* when you are exercising. When working out you should feel slightly breathless but not be gasping for air. Your body will start to tell you when you're working too hard:

- You'll start to get excessively hot
- You'll start to pant for breath
- Your muscles will start to ache more.

As you become used to exercising at the correct intensity, be aware of how your body feels. These feelings can educate you progressively about how your body responds to different exercise types. You will be surprised at how comfortable a reasonable workout intensity can feel to you once you get started. As you become more skilled at this you'll be able to accurately predict what your heart rate is without checking your monitor! Once you've reached this stage you'll be far more aware and in control of your body's response and better able to regulate your activity effectively. And, as you become fitter, there are different benefits to be obtained from working at different levels of intensity.

Time: How long should I exercise for in each session?

The simple answer to this question is for as long as you can fit it in and within the limits described in the Activity Continuum! Schedule the amount that fits into your lifestyle, start nice and slowly with 10 minutes and gradually extend this amount of time. As you become fitter and stronger you'll be able to do more. Keep it realistic, and you will achieve more in the long run. Think sensibly about the time it will take. You will gain more benefit from doing a number of short bouts of activity than you would from one prolonged session. The 20-, 40- and 60-minute guidelines of the Activity Continuum are guidelines only. Always bear in mind that if you can accumulate this much activity throughout a day (e.g. four bouts of five minutes' brisk walking), the benefits to your health will still be substantial. If your goals are health, well-being and weight loss you'll be moving in the right direction.

Think about how much time spent in each session would be right for you, now.

Type: What type of exercise is best?

Whether to do sports or exercise is the question that comes up for many people when starting any fitness regime. The answer is simply whatever you can stick to that will give you the desired result. A combination of the two may suit you ideally: perhaps some gym work and a game of golf, running and weight lifting, walking and swimming. But if you do want to incorporate any sporting activity into your routine, from football to jogging, remember the old maxim: 'Get fit to play sport; don't play sport to get fit'. In other words, trying to use sport as a way to get fit is a blunt instrument, as it will almost certainly not give you all-round fitness, so your performance in the sport will not be as good.

You have the parameters to assess your heart rate, so you need to find the combination that will work for you, and that you will find pleasurable and/or interesting enough to incorporate fully into your life.

How to Make Exercise Easier

You are embarking on a new way of life, the goal is to get fit in an achievable time-scale and to lose weight. You don't have to set any world records, or compare your progress to anyone else's. Here are some ways in which you can make it easy on yourself.

Be realistic

Don't set yourself up for goals that are unachievable. Take a look at the Activity Continuum (page 59) and move along one step at a time. Give yourself the chance to adapt to the new behaviours and, only when you are ready, move along to the next stage. One of the biggest causes of drop-out is always trying to do too much, too soon. Your company wouldn't grow from a corner shop to multinational grocery chain in one month, so why should you ask your body to transform from doing no activity to training like an Olympian in the same time?

Be efficient

Cut out all the wasted time. It is distance not time that determines energy used. If you run a mile in 7 minutes, you use no more energy than a person who takes 20 minutes to cover the same distance. The people who complete the marathon in 6 hours use exactly the same amount of energy as those who take $2\frac{1}{2}$ hours. If you're covering the same distance but reduce the time taken, then you're expending the same amount of energy as someone who took longer. Time is at a premium for most business executives, so think about how this could work for you.

- Could you exercise first thing in the morning? That way you save yourself the time and bother of showering, dressing and undressing twice a day.

- Have your exercise kit ready and in the same place each day, which means putting it there the night before, or immediately you have finished exercising. If you have two or three sets of exercise clothes that makes it even easier.

- Be flexible to help you to find unexpected opportunities for exercise. Take every opportunity to do a little more physical activity – walk up stairs, jog down the corridor, stretch at your desk – take advantage of any opportunity.

- Plan and be disciplined to stick to your body/business plan, just like you would in the office. Schedule exercise into your week. On a Sunday evening take a look at your goals for the coming week and put your activity times into the schedule. Be really reluctant to take them out. Your health will become your most important business asset, so treat looking after yourself as you would your most important business meeting.

- Finally, don't beat yourself up if your plans have to change. It just means they have to be changed, not abandoned. It's not an excuse to give up altogether.

Keeping a training log

The training log is obvious; you need a record of what you plan to do and how you did in comparison to the plan, just as you do for your business. Above all, recording and recognising your improvement is vitally important for motivation. It will note how much exercise you have done and where you didn't meet your target.

Also, you will need to put in your physical reactions, sickness, trembling muscles or the endorphin rush that makes you feel good. Note too if you have any injuries, however minor. If you should need to visit a physiotherapist, they will appreciate knowing how and when an injury may have started and how it may have built up over time. I sometimes take a note of the conditions when out running, whether wet, hot or windy, as they can be a factor that affects performance. Your personal trainer, if you decide to use one, will really appreciate being able to share this log with you.

It's essential that you have a record of your progress, and any areas of potential difficulty – either physically or mentally. You can make this a separate small book that you keep with your training kit, or as a separate section in your loose-leaf diary. (A training log comes with the Warriors Kit – see Useful Addresses, page 186.) You should record how much training you did, what sort of training it was, did you find it easy or difficult and how you felt about it. It's essential you just make a quick note at the time; do not put it off until later as you can rarely remember it in enough detail to be useful. A typical couple of days' entries, early on in the programme, might look like this (the tick indicates that the activity was carried out):

Planned	Actual	Mood and response
13 June		
20-minute jog	16 minutes and then walked	Got breathless and hot. Felt sick. Raining a bit, felt better – cooler.
Use stairs twice	Yes	Knees hurt, still strenuous for me
14 June		
Session with trainer: sit-ups, jog, weights programme	Increased sit-ups by 3. Didn't do enough weight reps	Very hard work, but felt was seeing improvement. Hate weights

The most useful aspect is that final column, as long as you are brutally honest about your response to the exercise, where you are feeling good and where it seemed like too much of a strain. On reviewing the log you will be struck by how there is invariably improvement in some area, even if it didn't feel like much at the time. You can re-read your log to give you inspiration and encouragement when you are flagging.

Making it easier on yourself

It is vitally important to find the right combination of things that you like doing, whether it's going to the gym, golf, dancing, walking or anything else. With dancing and many other sporting activities there is a social element to it too and when you can combine them that makes it a much richer experience.

Exercise can make you feel wonderful. One of the other things I would suggest is that if you're going for a particular sport, like for example, in my case, long- distance running, don't just see it as the grind of long-distance running, look at it from a completely different angle. I see it as an opportunity to indulge my love of the outdoors and nature. Or, if that's not for you, what about the pleasure that you derive from the company of others by playing a sport where you may enjoy being part of a team?

Key points

- Discover your true reasons for wanting to exercise

- Know where you are on the Wellness Continuum

- Establish your FITT principles

- Know where you can find out about your actual fitness level and plan to go there

- Know your desired outcome goals

- Know what your exercise requirements are and establish a time and plan that suits you

- Know your resting and maximum heart rate levels

- Look at the time management element of your exercise programme

- Set up an exercise log – and use it

- Know how to get the outside resources you need and where to find them

5
Business Plan II

Objectives

- To plan for your own body

- To find out what shape your body/business is
  in now

- To decide what you want out of your body/business

- To devise your own multi-stage Business Plan for
  weight management

As we have seen in Chapter 2 the Business Plan is possibly one of the most important business tools available. It is said that the majority of businesses that do not have a business plan fail. Make sure you and your body/business are not one of those failures!

The Language of the Business Plan

As a business executive, you are most probably used to succeeding in most things you put your mind to, but this area of weight management has had you stumped for some time. Yet managing your body is no different to managing a business. If you have the skills for one you can easily transfer them to the other. But, as we have already seen, most of the weight-loss programmes around are just not geared up to the needs of executives.

The language of the Business Plan is very suitable for the Warriors programme, and makes an ideal model, offering a way of communicating to the male business executive that is easy to relate to and draws on many of the skills you already possess.

If you are an overweight male, you will know that it can be an isolating experience. Do you sometimes think, for example, that you cannot share your feelings because that would be dropping your guard? Do you also sense that to do so would not be manly? You are not alone. Plenty of men feel that way. Sometimes there is a feeling that you are bigger and stronger and people can't push you around when you're overweight. So, if you start trying to lose weight that 'protection' disappears. What you need to do is find the confidence to let that guard relax a bit, and feel comfortable in sharing your experiences, if you wish. That was how the Warriors courses started. It is a very male-focused, male-driven organisation, but at the same time a place where men can feel confident in expressing what they are going through on their weight management issues. (If you are interested in finding out more about these courses, visit the Warriors website – see Useful Addresses, page 186.)

The ability to stand back from yourself, to view yourself almost as a different person, is a skill that can be acquired and is one that is common to many successful executives. Think of yourself as your imaginary business consultant, as you embark on the Warriors programme, with you as a new client. Think about what that consultant would see. Think about the things that would go through his mind if he were looking at you. And think about what he might say to you. Bear in mind, his job is to get the very best out of you.

When first devising the Warriors programme, I realised that managing your weight is like managing any other business. It's a question of focus and discipline, it's a question of setting goals and objectives and finding strategies in order to take you there. So I started to develop my own thinking about how I could make the body a business and put it in a language that executives can genuinely understand.

Prioritising Your New Business

If a man says to me that he doesn't have time to exercise, my response is usually to say: 'Well, I understand, I mean in your day-to-day work you definitely don't, but if your boss said to you, "Congratulations! You've got your promotion – you've just been given a new division to run, you can run that with your present responsibilities!", would you turn round to him and say, "Sorry, I don't have time to do that, I'm just too busy to handle any more work!"?'

Invariably, I would then receive a startled look and the man would immediately say that in those circumstances of course he would find the time! Exactly right, of course he would. That is what we do when given a promotion with new responsibilities, and all the benefits that go with it – we manage it. Well, this time that other division or company is yourself. It needs to be given that priority. You need to make it just as important as any other new venture, because if that venture fails it can bring the whole business to a standstill.

That is how the Business Plan concept started to evolve. Not only because I saw it was a very good fit, but it started to answer a lot of the issues and questions. When it is addressed in that way people with an executive lifestyle begin to say 'Aha' and the penny drops. What the man in the example above is actually saying is, 'I choose not to have the time and it's because I don't rate it high in the scale of priorities.'

> What you need to understand to make this programme work, is that you can manage your body like you can manage your business. You have to see your body as an outside entity that you are actually managing.

Of course, many successful executives are extremely good at running their business, and no doubt you are too. You understand how to do it and have the skills. You are practised at it. But there is one aspect of your life that you've never been able to control, which is your eating, drinking and weight management. Does that sound familiar?

Now, if you just shift all of the experience that you have had from running a business, into running your body, you will suddenly realise that you already have the skills to do the job. For instance, you have the skills to cope with the culture change required in weight management, because those skills are required in business. You also know that you need to set out on the basis of working out 'What is this company about?'.

As with any company, one of the first things you need to do is to set a strategy – have a plan. But the plan has to be based on something. True, you may have little experience of running this particular business – your body – but you do know how to run a business and can apply some of the tried-and-tested ways of doing that. There are two key questions that we will keep coming back to while setting your strategy. The first is 'What shape is the business in now?', while the second is 'What do you want out of your business?'.

What Shape is the Business in Now?

Previous chapters have looked at the health and nutritional checks you need to make, so you now are aware of how important it is to know what your stock levels are – in other words, what is your weight? How efficient is your plant and machinery, is your body running smoothly or are there areas that need some specific help? For example, what's the level of your blood pressure, what's your level of cholesterol?

This is rather like going round the factory and seeing how operationally efficient it is. Is there some faulty machinery, can it be repaired, reconditioned, mended? So, for example, you may have a knee problem or an ankle problem, and you know what you can do to alleviate that. It may not be possible to do anything at all. You may have some old machinery in the factory (perhaps an arthritic knee), and you may not have the resources with which to recondition it (an expensive orthopaedic operation), but it is an essential part of the factory. So you'll do the best you can at getting that knee into as good a shape as possible. Your machinery – your body – may not be the most up-to-date model on the market, but it can be much improved. In many cases improvement, particularly in muscle strength and tone, can be very rapid.

What Do You Want Out of Your Business?

Do you just want to drive down stock levels – i.e. lose weight – or have you a goal in mind? You might just want to be able to walk the dog without getting breathless, or play a round of golf every week, or even run in a marathon. Whatever it is, you need to be clear about your objectives now, before you start. So you are going to take your reading on your body/business, and then assess where you want that business to go. All these skills are second nature to a good businessman.

Starting to Plan

(*You will need to get out your notebook and something to write with before reading on.*)

Begin by thinking of your body as an independent company. It's not one you have managed before, but suddenly you have been given a promotion and your boss has told you the good news – you are about to take on some additional duties – you have a new business to run. If you are an entrepreneur, or a CEO, imagine your body is the business you have just acquired in your latest takeover. With any new business there are some important questions to be answered. You need information, facts upon which to plan your strategy for your new venture. Let's look at the components of our Business Plan individually. When reading through the rest of this chapter you will want to make notes – it's part of your research and development tool. Start by thinking about the following:

How to Look at Your Body/Business

There are three stages in the production cycle of any company, which are equally applicable to your body/business.

Before

The 'before' stage covers incoming supplies: the supermarket, the restaurants, those who prepare food or cook for you at home. What you're trying to analyse here is whether their supply is appropriate to the needs of your body/business. Very good salesmen, like those at Haagen Daz, McDonald's and Guinness, will be trying to sell you wonderfully attractive products, which you would love to buy, but they may not be appropriate to your needs.

This 'before' stage also encompasses the planning and strategic review. Here you look at what shape the business is in and what you want to do with it. You also decide if there is any other equipment you may need for your body/business. Do you need kitchenware, for example, or some sports equipment? Do you need some measuring tools – scales, tape measure, even an extra notch on your belt? Do you need some form of record to monitor progress? All these things have been covered in previous chapters, so you should already have a clear idea of your specific requirements.

During

The 'during' stage covers production. It looks at what fuel is required and what stock is needed to keep the factory going – in other words, what are the levels of nutrition?

It also looks at how to keep motivation high – man management. Additionally it includes areas such as culture change and a suitable benefits package for the team managing the business. If you translate this into your body/business, then it is all about how to keep your 'support team' on side. Also, consider whether the equipment is up to standard. Does it need maintenance and improvement? Are there any joints that have special needs? Do you need to lower blood pressure or cholesterol?

What other medical issues need to be addressed so that the body can function at its optimal level?

After

Finally – and this is the really important part – you need to ask, what do you want to produce? That is what the company is there for – to produce goods or services. What do you really want your body to do for you? Look at what you really want to do, physically, and then decide what you need to do to get there, by working back to the 'during' or production phase and from that working out how much 'before', or supplies, you really need and the appropriate volume and mix that is required. (see the table on page 76).

How does the table apply to you? Start by looking at the After section, and note down **now**, what you really want out of your body. Later on you will have enough information to fill in the Before and During stages. But, for now, just write down what you want out of your body!

Putting Your Business Plan Together

Your Business Plan is divided into 18 sections, which will be personal to you. Each section is like an individual chapter in your plan and needs to be fully developed, on paper, by you. The following sections are there to guide you into what you need to consider when completing each section.

1. What's the history?

The way to start a Business Plan is to look at the history of the business. It's a question of taking a snapshot of where you are starting from. There are all kinds of key things to tease out from your background:

* What have been the ups?
* What have been the downs?
* What can you learn from the past?

Before	During	After
Everything that happens before it goes into your body/business	Everything that happens in your body/business	The outcomes What you really want to produce from your body/business
Suppliers: e.g. Supermarkets and restaurants Partners/significant others	**Mind-set:** Motivation to do the job and to keep going	**Health:** e.g. lower blood pressure
Medical Examination: e.g. full check-up	**Nutrition:** How much and what sort	**Sport:** e.g. play golf twice weekly
Planning: The Business Plan The Picture in Words	**Exercise:** How much do I need and how often When am I going to do it Also look at what condition the equipment is in and if any maintenance needs to be done	**Looks and agility** e.g. lose 2 stones in weight
Preparation: The right equipment for the job	**Management:** Includes culture changes, team building, motivation and rewards	**Strength and stamina:** e.g. climb stairs easily Carry shopping/ luggage
		Energy levels e.g. not feel sleepy after lunch

- How did you reach this point?
- What has brought you here?
- When did you decide to do something?
- Why did you decide to do something?

What can you learn from your past history? Have you tried to lose weight before and, if so, what worked and what didn't work for you? Look at where you can build on your strengths. And look at where you can overcome some of the weaknesses. Having a medical check-up is an excellent idea, to get a reading on where your body/business stands and, what's going on. Is it high blood pressure, is it cholesterol, is it aching joints? What are the factors that give you a really good picture of where you are now?

2. A SWOT analysis

If you were running a business, and putting a Business Plan in place, you would undertake a SWOT exercise – *do one on yourself*. Think about yourself under these four headings:

- Strengths
- Weaknesses
- Opportunities
- Threats.

List out the factors in each category to help you to get to know where you need support, where you can really be strong and how to select the best team to give you the support that will be helpful. Here are some examples to get you thinking:

> • **Strengths:** Are you highly focused and disciplined? Once you commit to something, do you always see it through to the end? Do you enjoy a particular sport and would you be willing to play more and at a higher level? Are you a brilliant time-manager, always able to deal with important issues?

- **Weaknesses:** Do you find that, no matter how much discipline you have, there is an internal dialogue that always seems to defeat you – 'Just one more won't do me any harm'? Or do you just love to have a drink and a snack to unwind before dinner, as you come home from work?

- **Opportunities:** How can you do two things at once – exercise and be with the family or friends at the same time? How can you plan ahead on a business trip so that you stay at a hotel that gives you access to sport and the right type of food? Can you get your PA or your travel agent to book a healthy eating option on your next flight?

- **Threats:** Do you have eating or drinking buddies who are close friends and somehow always manage to get you going out for a few pints and a curry? Do you have colleagues at work who can eat anything and not put on weight – so they always have biscuits and cakes in the office? Or do you and your partner always have fun going out to try new restaurants – that is just one of your great pleasures in life?

3. The product

It is important to take a second look at what you want from your body because you have to be absolutely certain that you know what that is. Look at what you have previously written and consider again whether it is what you really want.

In this case the product is your dream of what you want to be physically. So, what is your outcome, what are you in business to do? In other words, look at the end of the process. What do you actually want your body to be able to do for you?

- What are your initial thoughts about this new business?
- Does it have potential?
- What sort of potential, exactly?
- What sort of shape is it in now?
- What do I know about its management?
- What do I know about its systems?
- Can it perform to the standards I will set for it?
- What can I expect from it?

4. The marketing strategy

The next thing to tackle is the marketing strategy. Key questions here are:

- Who do you need to sell this concept to?
- Are they going to be supportive?
- Do you need to advertise?

If you have never undertaken any weight-loss programme before, or you are just starting to think about changing your habits, you are more or less building the prototype and perhaps it's too early to let anyone know what you are doing. You need to consider at what stage you should involve other people in this process. There may be some people who are very close to you, like family and friends, that need advertising and marketing to persuade them that this is the course that you want to take. Sell them the benefits so they don't feel threatened, but can see how it might enrich their relationship with you. Then there are others like colleagues and employees whom you may not want to know what you are about to do. In marketing terms, the product is under wraps, you haven't got to the final model yet, so what you are trying to do is build this prototype that is top secret. However, you will need to involve a core team, so work out who needs to know.

5. Market research

Do you need to do some market research, particularly in the area of social relationships? For example, do you have regular eating and drinking buddies or work colleagues whom you meet up with in the pub? You may have a wife or a partner who has become your best friend in going out to restaurants, or perhaps you find yourself planning a holiday around a destination where the cuisine is known to be wonderful. You need to think very carefully about what the consequences are when starting this sort of process and how to handle the cultural change.

You may also have to do market research around how you are going to build your support team. Who is your support team going to be and what does it consist of? For advice on mind-set and exercise coaches, and nutritionists, look in the Useful Addresses section on page 186 and visit the Warriors website.

6. How the business is run

You owe it to your body to run it efficiently and effectively. This part of your Business Plan is all about your day-to-day activities and how they are going to be managed. Look at how you apportion your time, and how you work through the day. In other words, consider how your body/business is run. The business has to be run in the context of all the other things you are doing and it means looking at these areas first. So, think about how you spend your day.

- Are there any spare moments in the day that could be freed up right now, to manage your new body/business?
- Can you get up a little earlier?
- Is it possible to leave work say an hour sooner?
- Could you combine sport and being with the family – so that you can do both at the same time?

To take a different tack:

- If none of the above were possible, think about it in the context of running a new business – where would you allocate time from your present day to accommodate it?

- Would you be able to delegate more of the work to others, as you would if you had a new division or business to run?
- If so, what would you delegate and to whom?

How much time you will need to free up will depend on what you want to achieve from your body and in what time frame. The absolute key element here is looking at your life as it is right now. How are you going to slot this business of running your body into everything else that's going on in your life? To do that you need to consider how you will leave enough time for the following:

- regular exercise
- meal planning
- shopping for healthy options
- cooking or preparing meals
- spending 'review' time on your progress.

7. Management structure

Management is something that any good investor or lender to the business would always be interested in – so would the person in charge of the company. Your question here is 'Are you the only management in the business?'. One single person running a business is actually self-employed. If you find that the same applies to the management of your body, you may need to think a bit wider. Ask yourself if you need other people in your body/business, whether they can help you and what kind of help they can give.

You could use your SWOT analysis (pages 77–78), as a guide, to point you in the direction of the team that may be able to help you achieve the aims and objectives of the business. In your Business Plan, write something like this and fill in the blanks for your particular situation:

- The main risks are...

- To minimise the risks I need to...

- I plan to do this by...(time or date).

- The type of support I need is... (this is whatever you've analysed it to be and you need to show how this support will help overcome the weaknesses you've identified)

- I have significant opportunities to...

- The support (list or quantify that support) will enable me to... (whatever it is you want to do)

- In return for this support I shall (give the stated outcome that you want)...

Who is on your team?

You could decide you require external support from consultants or that you need to join the Warriors programme (see Useful Addresses, page 186). Can you count on your partner, friends, family, colleagues and professional support? Are they all motivated? Have they bought into your vision? What will each person bring to the business? What is their experience and skill and qualifications? What will your team get out of it? One benefit to them could be you becoming a better person, for example, or a more compatible person or a healthier person.

You need to see what benefits there are to your team for doing this. Clearly, if you are employing consultants, such as a personal trainer, there is a financial benefit. That does not mean to say that they might not feel satisfied when you've achieved your goals – they may get huge personal satisfaction out of it, but recognising these aspects is very important. Although your team is there to support you, it's a two-way process, and you need to give them feedback too. They need some encouragement occasionally to give the best of themselves. As a good business manager, you understand that. The interplay between you and your team is an important factor in your success. Do not underestimate the difference a good team can make!

8. Who is the competition?

All businesses need to know who their main competitors are, who could sabotage their market and their plans. Your body is the company here, and your competitors are going to be both external and internal. What factors are going to divert you from your objectives? The external ones are easier to spot. It may be your drinking and eating buddies or your partner who are competing for your time and attention. They don't want you to break social habits like drinking in the bar after work or having a rich and calorific celebration dinner with lots of champagne and double brandies. You need to look at this from all angles so, going wider still, is your job your main competitor? This could be because of the pressures of overwork or too much travel not allowing you sufficient time to manage your body properly to achieve your goals.

The internal competitors are usually more subtle – they are the ingrained habits of self-sabotage. 'Just one drink won't make any difference' or 'I have had a lousy day so I am treating myself to a really good night out'. Or what about when it's cold and wet, so you don't want to go for a run? You overslept so you haven't time to do your normal routine; you have to finish a major report so there is no time to go to the gym. Putting your self-care first is not usually a high priority, and every time you back off from your new regime, you are sabotaging yourself. So ask yourself, what are the things that are competing against your business for its time, for its culture, for its perspective and what it really wants to achieve?

9. SMART goal setting

One of the first things most people think about for their Business Plan is to write out the goals, targets and milestones that they want to achieve. In business terminology, goals need to be SMART in order for you to achieve your objectives.

A SMART goal is:

Specific

Measurable

Achievable

Realistic

Time-related

Your goal may be to lose 4 stones in a year, but obviously that is not something you can do overnight. You've got to do it in small stepping stones, and the same applies to pretty much any objective you set, either for your company or for your body. So the classic way of doing this is by breaking that goal down into small stepping stones to get you along the route to your final destination. Set yourself a first target for one month and a second target for three months. You know these are within reach, pretty much. They may stretch you a little, but you can still just about get there. Remember too to include your specific goals on daily calories and exercise that you set in Chapters 3 and 4 respectively, as these are core goals for your body/business and should not be omitted.

Relate this to your goal of losing 4 stones over a year. Does it fit the SMART criteria? It is specific. It is measurable, in small stages, of losing no more than 1 per cent of your body weight in a week. It is certainly achievable, because you know that if you are taking in the right amount of calories, the right nutrition and the necessary amount of exercise, that it can be done. Is it realistic? Absolutely it's realistic. You won't damage your system if you're losing under 1 per cent of your body weight a week, so you've got a healthy, steady weight loss. And you have a time frame in which to operate. In a month you know that you should have, more or less, achieved a 4 per cent drop in weight.

> Ask yourself: what are the three main goals you want to achieve from this programme and in what time-scale do you want to get there?

If one of your goals is weight loss, it is crucial to know how you are going to measure that. What yardsticks will you use? Are you looking at weight loss in terms of pounds or kilos, inches or centimetres? Or are you going to use a different standard and gauge it by your fitness level or ability to compete in sports? Or you could choose to measure it against your health factors, such as heart rate, blood pressure, cholesterol levels or by the specific date by when you wanted to achieve any of these things. It is probably better to set yourself an overall goal and work towards that, because although weight loss serves as a good measure, it is not always easy to set it as a time-related goal, since your body does not always respond to weight loss on a direct linear basis. It's often more like a zigzag pattern on a graph.

You are treating your body like a business: you wouldn't look at your profit and loss statement every five minutes to find out whether you are in profit, so don't do that with your body either. Instead, take monthly reviews, or quarterly reviews, whatever suits you best. Or get a good reading on the number of calories eaten per day or the minutes of aerobic exercise taken per day, because those are the things that are much more easily within your remit and control, and you can make sure you get a real focus on them.

10. Essential equipment

Accurate record keeping gives you a real sense of your achievements. Before you start the Warriors programme you need to decide what measuring tools you want to employ. If you have been through the earlier chapters of this book, you should already have put together your own training log and Food and Mood Diary.

The training log is obvious; you need a record of what you plan to do and how you did in comparison to your plan. Above all, recording and recognising your improvement is vitally important for motivation. You will note how much exercise you have done and where you didn't meet your target or, indeed, where you exceeded expectations.

The Food and Mood Diary records what you plan to eat and drink, and then notes everything you ate and drank, and in what quantity so you have an accurate calorie check of your daily intake – like the profit and loss account of a company. The Mood part of the diary is where you record your emotional response to and triggers for food, and that then enables you to see the patterns that may exist and what you can do to become more successful.

11. Counting the cost

Any Business Plan has to allow for the expenditure needed to start or revitalise a company. Undertaking a weight management programme has some genuine financial costs, which should be built into your profit and loss account. Consider the costs of some of these:

- Exercise equipment – treadmill, rowing machine, bicycle, weights, rebounder, videos
- New clothing – running shoes, shorts, track suit

- Additional cooking equipment – wok, steamer
- Training facilities – gym, swimming pool, sports club membership
- Training budget – nutritionist, personal trainer, mind-set coach
- Time costs for programme and review
- Monitoring equipment – scales, tape measure, full-length mirror
- Record-keeping notebooks – training log, Food and Mood Diary

12. Making time for change

This process takes time. You may be thinking – 'I don't see how I can fit all this extra planning and monitoring into my life'. My answer is to ask yourself, if you were managing a new business for at least the next three years, how would you manage it? The answer most businessmen would give would probably be along the lines of needing to find ways of delegating more. If you have genuine time constraints you need to look around your own resources, or look to see what resources you can build in, which would give you the support in the areas that were deficient. Of course there are key essentials that are non-negotiable and can't be delegated because they absolutely have to be done by you. Exercise is one area you won't be able to delegate, but food shopping, preparation and cooking could possibly be handed over to someone else. For other aspects of time management, look at Chapter 9.

13. Role models

Good managers compare themselves company to company, not person to person, in other words they look at how their company is placed in comparison to the competition. Generally, you would aim to be in the top quartile of your particular industry. Weight management is similar. Do you have any successful role models for weight loss and general fitness? What are the things that they do that make them successful? Ask yourself, 'Who has done well at what I want to do?' and see if you can use that person as a role model to improve your understanding of the process (look at Chapter 8 on self-image for more on how to do this).

14. Undertaking a cost/benefit analysis

This is a very useful tool that relates to some of the things we've already discussed. A cost/benefit analysis means looking at how much you have to expend, in terms of capital in your business, relative to the outcome and the benefits you're going to receive, in terms of profit. Relating that to undertaking the Warriors programme means looking at the cost in terms of your relationships, whether it's with your partner or your friends, and what it might literally cost you in terms of those relationships. If you are not willing to join colleagues in a takeaway from a fast-food restaurant when you are working late, or switch to slimline tonic on your regular night out at the pub, what might that cost you? Look at your programme in terms of exercise and what it might cost you, say, in physical exertion, and then weigh that against the benefits that you will receive from it, in terms of a fitter and healthier body – that's part of your cost/benefit analysis. Is this a price you consider well worth paying?

15. Looking at the consequences

What consequences will you face if the plan for your body/business does not succeed? In business, the consequences of failure are considerable and pretty well instant. You could have your bank manager and creditors hounding you on the telephone, threatening legal action. You may have shareholders who are going to remove you from running the business, or the boss is giving you a hard time and you might lose your job.

The difficulty with managing your body/business is that the consequences are never that clear, and often the issues can be dodged quite easily. Yet, the long-term consequences can be just as stark, and just as serious. The difficulty of trying to gauge what the consequences might be is one of the key factors in assessing your actions. What you need to do is try to build in consequences that are hopefully internally driven, though sometimes it is necessary to build some external ones too, if you want to achieve the success you desire. Here are some points to consider, when thinking about, and noting down, the consequences of not following through on your Warriors programme.

Companies, and more especially the management in those companies, are responsible to their shareholders. Clearly you yourself are a major shareholder in your body. In fact, you are the majority shareholder. You could argue the point, however, that you have other shareholders too, such as your partner, your children or even your business. As the manager and CEO of your body/business you are responsible to those shareholders and need to take them into consideration.

You really do have to look at both internal and external consequences. You need to be working on internal self-respect and self-esteem. Your fear factors, such as a heart attack, or lack of mobility, are important too. The pleasure factors, the vision of what you will be, are all-important internal driving forces and are much more important than the externally driven forces. Yes, the external driving forces will help you, but they can always be taken away one way or another at random, and they may only be temporary. If you find the internal driving forces and consequences, that's where you really get your inner strength from.

When you focus on the consequences of not following through on the Warriors programme, these are the key questions to ask yourself:

- How much do you respect the opinions of your partner, doctor or coaches?
- How much do you respect yourself?
- How much do you really care if you succeed?
- What are your values, relative to where you are now?
- What sort of things do you want out of your life that you are not getting because of the way you are living now?

By answering these questions you will be building in consequences for yourself. You have to find the things that will push you, if you do not succeed in following through with your plans. For example, challenging yourself to undertake a sponsored weight loss is a method that works for some people. That puts you very much in the public domain. You might also look at your mission statement (see below) or an abbreviated version of your current short-term goal, to remind you of the consequences of not following through.

16. Premises and equipment

Is your kitchen ready for your weight management programme? Start with a general clear-out. Just like a company take-over, you are going to get rid of the obsolete machinery, tidy things up, get things into shape. Here's a checklist to get you started:

- Clear the kitchen cupboards of everything unhealthy.
- Check the labels of what you do keep for calories, sugar and fat content.
- Ditch instant and convenience foods that are not nutritious and low-calorie.
- Clear the fridge of cream, butter, full-fat cheeses, pâtés and salamis.
- No stores of biscuits, sweets or chocolate – not even for cooking.
- Check the freezer; get rid of ice-creams and desserts or gateaux.
- Remove the alcohol unless you really can resist it.

It's not all throwing away; there are some things you may also want to add. You are going to be more adventurous about your food and your kitchen can reflect that. If you are not already a cook, do you need to get some extra help with some specialist training? If you do, then where will you go and what sort of additional skills will you need?

Things to add to your kitchen

- Low-fat snacks and sauces

- Low-calorie drinks and foods

- A range of herbs and spices

- A steamer and a wok

- Some good low-fat, low-calorie cookbooks (see
  Further Reading, page 195)

Premises can also include any space you might want to use at home for exercise. Is it clear enough for you to move around in? If you have a portable gym or rowing machine, are they in good working order? If you are using weights, have you got enough space to operate safely?

17. Break-even analysis

This again is a familiar business concept. It's rather like an equation: on the top line of a fraction you would have over-heads, then underneath that line you would have gross profit margins. On the other side you would have times one hundred which equals the break-even of sales.

$$\frac{\text{Overheads}}{\text{Gross profit margins}} \times 100 = \text{break-even sales}$$

Overheads

In terms of weight management, this is the price you're going to pay for doing it and it's the cost both in terms of time, money and emotion. That might mean the financial resources you use to buy in the team that you need or the possible change in your relationships, as you face the fact that you and your partner will no longer be able to share in those frequent, deeply indulgent restaurant meals.

Gross profit margin

These are the benefits that you are getting out of undertaking the programme – weight loss, increased health, vitality and fitness, and many others, including more energy and a better frame of mind. Benefits could also be financial, as you may be spending less on food generally and on eating out in particular. It may also mean less spent on medication and time with the doctor. You may also feel better about yourself. Think of all the good you will derive from managing this enterprise – your body/business – successfully.

Break-even point of sale

This is your balance between the price you are prepared to pay – 'overheads' – and the benefits you derive – 'gross profit margin'. You are the one who decides where the break-even point should rest. Life is about balances and 'shades of grey' – it is not always clearly black or white – and, when managing your body/business, the same rules apply. Take a note of the price you are prepared to pay for the profit of a healthy, fit body.

18. The final stages

An **executive summary** usually accompanies any good Business Plan and condenses and focuses into one page what the whole thing is about. Doing an executive summary is important. It gives you real clarity and it shakes down exactly what you want for your business and what you think it's all about.

A **mission statement** is also something to develop at this stage. Many companies have mission statements that get tucked away in a drawer. Even the CEO doesn't always know what the hell the mission statement says. But a good mission statement can be a bit like a mantra that you can quote back to yourself at any point. It should be reinforcing and give you inner strength, to focus you back on to what you really want to do. If you can summarise in a few words what you're really about and what you're trying to achieve, then, when things get tough, you can quote that back as your own personal motto and that can be enough to bring you back on track. For example, the mission statement for my company, Warriors, is:

> To empower and inspire men to achieve their optimum health and fitness so they can perform at their peak and derive the most from their lives.

Or, to use the shorthand version:

> Mentally strong – physically fit.

Once you have drawn up your Business Plan and executive summary, you are ready to get into the details that make the Warriors programme work.

Key points

- Managing your body is like managing any other business and you have the skills already.

- Remember the production cycle: before, during, after.

- Know your SMART goals and make sure they reflect your true needs, particularly in the areas of nutrition and exercise.

- Get yourself organised for what you need at work and home, especially for exercise and nutrition.

- Consider the true costs of undertaking your new programme and ensure you are comfortable with them in all areas.

- Produce your executive summary and then develop your personal mission statement, making sure it's memorable, short and reflects what your 'body/business' is really about.

6
A Picture in Words

Objectives
• To learn ways in which to boost your motivation and when to use them
• To express truthfully how you feel about yourself before starting to lose weight
• To express how your future life will be once you have lost weight and improved your fitness
• To visualise your bright new future

When you have lost weight and things are going really well, complacency often sets in. That's when temporary, and sometimes permanent, failure can occur. A major asset that can help you avoid this pitfall is for you to 'paint a picture in words', capturing your current mood and thinking, on paper, right now.

In order to do this, you are going to examine the reality of where you are right now. Whatever your motivation for buying and reading this book, an honest assessment of your physical and emotional state, at this moment, will sustain you and support you in the future. Your personal Picture in Words is a very important document that you will want to refer to, so keep it somewhere safe.

You might want to make notes first before you write the actual 'picture', or read to the end of the chapter for some ideas or inspiration, or you may just want to go straight in. Whatever method you choose, you need to go deep inside yourself and, being totally honest, express on paper exactly how you feel about your weight. I describe in detail later in the chapter how to actually get started, but here are some things to consider when undertaking this process:

- What is your weight doing to you and your life?

- Why do you *absolutely have to change?*

- What are the things you cannot currently do that you would love to be doing if you were the size and shape you aim to become? Describe them in detail.

- Look at the damage your weight is doing to you, and your life, right now. How does that make you feel?

- What is the absolutely worst thing about being overweight for you?

This is not an exercise in self-flagellation; it is designed to be a strong motivator. This is something that is useful now, and becomes invaluable in the future. I promise you that the deeper you can go and the more honest you can be with yourself now about why you really want to change, the more valuable your Picture in Words will become, in the future.

Why Look Back?

At some point in the Warriors programme, when you have got fitter, healthier and lost weight, you may well have difficulty remembering exactly how things were right at the beginning and will feel complacent. What you will be getting from undertaking this exercise is a much higher level of self-nurture and self-understanding. By knowing what causes you to be overweight, and how you can combat it, you gain greater self-respect, self-discipline, and a great sense of achievement. But a crucial part of that process is knowing exactly what your starting point is.

For example, my own Picture in Words contained all the worst aspects of being so desperately overweight. I expressed, as clearly as I could, all that was going through my mind at that time. At 22 stone (140 kg), the physical toll it was taking on me was high: I suffered with lower back pain, aching feet, breathlessness. Chairs were an embarrassment. Aeroplane seats were uncomfortable. There was the painful realisation that I had wasted much of my life, which could have been so much better. Girlfriends and relationships were out of the question because I was far too embarrassed about my body. Particularly strong for me was the feeling of self-loathing at how low I had allowed myself to slide. I expressed my feelings of misery at what I had become and how there didn't seem to be any way out.

Here are some of the things I put into my Picture in Words from the notes I made at the time:

- Hard to travel – airline and train seats too narrow

- Not safe – can't do up seat belts on cars or planes

- Difficulty dressing – can't get my socks and shoes on

- Social embarrassment – will the chair hold my weight?

- Restricted social life – won't go swimming, can't play golf or tennis

- Risks to my health – lack of energy, potential heart problems

- Buying clothes – more expensive and hate looking in the mirror

- No relationships – embarrassed to be seen naked

This Picture in Words was a permanent reminder of what it had really felt like and ensured that I would always be motivated never to return there again. It was something that was very deep and very powerful – something that had the strength to invoke a change in my habits and my way of life. I had already come to the conclusion that I wasn't happy where I was in my life. I needed to understand clearly why that was, in order to do something about it. That was a **fundamental part of the process**.

Your Own Picture in Words

Write down your own picture, of who you are and where you are, right now. It is essential you do so *before* you embark on any of the exercise or nutritional parts of the programme. Once there has been some improvement in your physical well-being, your attitude and mind-set will change very rapidly, and it becomes almost impossible to recapture how you really felt at the outset of the programme. The pain or anguish that you feel now – that readiness for change – will not last! But it can be a vital driving force. One that, if you can capture it in words now, will keep you motivated in a really powerful way.

These are the issues you should consider:

- **How do you feel, physically?** Do you have low energy? Are there things that you cannot do because of your weight – like playing sport or even just going for a walk?

- **Are there any medical reasons why you must lose weight?** For example, is your blood pressure too high? Do you have diabetes? Is high cholesterol a problem?

- **Are you in pain because of your weight?** Do your joints hurt? Are there areas of your body that would benefit from weight reduction? Does your back give you problems – is this weight-related?

- **How do you feel about your weight?** Are you embarrassed to go swimming? Are you worried that people look at you as someone who is overweight? Do you dislike what you see in the mirror?

- **What damage is being done to your life by being overweight?** Is it restricting your lifestyle? Is it putting you at risk? Is it affecting your relationship with your partner? Is it holding you back at work?

- **What are the consequences to you, and the people who matter most to you, if you do not do something about your weight?** What could happen to your wife and children? What could happen to your business? What will happen to your life? What will happen as you become older?

Refining the picture

Once you have written down your Picture in Words you can use a further technique to keep you focused and motivated for much longer. Every day you look for one more *original* reason why you absolutely have to do this programme, and note that down. For the first few days that will be easy, but after about a month you will probably run out of original ideas. This exercise focuses you very strongly on looking for reasons why you *really* want to change and that will take you through the most difficult stage – starting the change.

Research shows that a new habit is formed after 21 repetitions. At that stage it is still very slender, but there, nevertheless. So, when you embark on this programme, much energy and effort is expended in getting those new habits in place. It is not always comfortable. One way to work through these tough times is to maintain your focus. Writing down your Picture in Words and thinking of new, original ideas of why you really want to change, will see you through this initial process. Once the first few weeks have elapsed you will have already built some new habits. If you continue to foster those new habits the process starts to become easier.

Remember your first day at the office? Everything was new. It was exciting, perhaps, but uncomfortable. You were experiencing change. Weight management is a similar process. But like all change, once it becomes a habit, you begin to wonder what the fuss was all about.

To use the analogy of the rocket launch: think of the rocket on its base, waiting for launch into outer space. Then think of the take-off. Huge amounts of vapour and flames are thrown out from the base. There is a terrific expenditure of energy and the rocket has only lifted a few feet off the ground. Then gradually there is acceleration. The rocket moves away from the ground at ever-increasing speed. By the time it has travelled a few thousand feet the booster rockets are jettisoned. Suddenly it is moving faster and using less energy, as it breaks through the atmosphere and earth's gravitational pull. Your Warriors weight management programme is a similar process.

The Warriors 'rocket launch'

Once you have written down your own Picture in Words, keep it handy, so you can regularly refer back to it when you need some encouragement to go on, or some feedback on what you have already accomplished. After you have written your document and embarked on the Warriors programme, you will find your perspective of how bad things were will change – thank goodness! Any improvement makes us forget the original state of affairs. In my case, I was initially focused strongly on the medical side, because risk of injury was where my greatest concern lay. Because I wanted to take up sports again, I obviously had to be very careful about how I set about it. One of the things I wrote in my own document was that my feet hurt when walking. After a few months I was walking quite long distances and when I read that again, I found it hard to remember that I could barely walk a City block without being in pain. But re-reading that comment was a terrific sign to me of how much progress I had made overall. That's why this document is so important.

Building the dream

This is part two of the process. You have identified all the reasons why you *absolutely have to lose weight*. Now you are going to really visualise what you want to lose that weight for, and how different your life will become when you have succeeded. In other words, what does your new life look like – the one that you dream of it becoming?

It is time to take a few more notes. This time it's not a list of what's wrong with your way of life, but it is a positive statement of what you want to achieve from the Warriors programme, and your new life. What do you really want? Spend time visualising what you want and how your body can help you to fulfil your dreams, your ambitions, your hopes and your aspirations. Start by looking at the things you really enjoy in life and what involvement your body might have in that process:

- Would you really like to play a better game of tennis, walk further, run up and down stairs, have a lower cholesterol level, lower blood pressure, no back pain?

- What are the things that are going to make a difference to improving the quality of your life?

- What are the pleasurable things that you want to do, where a healthier body is essential in order to achieve them?

Once you can focus on what those things are, they pull you forward in a way where everything else becomes a natural consequence. If you can think: 'If I have the cream buns or I have the glasses of wine to excess, I won't be able to play football with the kids, or go on a skiing holiday with my friends.' Then you can go on to think: 'But, if I change my way of approaching food and make a positive choice to reduce my calorie intake, then my dream of being able to do those things – things that give me huge pleasure, things that I want to be able to do – can become a reality.'

> Make your vision of the future compelling.
> Make it something that is a source of rich pleasure
> each time your mind turns towards it.

Before you put pen to paper to write down your positive thoughts, imagine how good life will be. See yourself as the proud owner of a body you have always wanted. Feel the same joy that you experience when your company has gone from rags to riches, or you have been able to successfully pull off a difficult deal or merger.

Visualisation

In business, and in many other areas, the technique of 'visualisation' is used to elicit the essence of a desire to do or have something, in the future. You can follow the suggested technique below, or use whatever visualisation method you find works best for you.

Read right through this section at least once – and some people find it helpful to go through it a couple of times – before first attempting the visualisation. It might even be helpful for you to record the instructions on to a tape and play it back, leaving space for your thoughts. When you are ready, find a quiet time, when you can relax and be on your own for about 30–40 minutes. Make sure that the phone will not ring and that no one will disturb you. Sit, or lie down, whichever way is most comfortable for you, and relax. Give yourself a minute or two to settle down, and clear your mind of any day-to-day worries or thoughts. Take a few deep breaths, inhaling and exhaling very gently and very deeply. Let your body sink into the surrounding area and let your mind go blank. In this totally relaxed state, gradually focus your mind on a point in the future. One where you would like to be when you have overcome all your current weight and health-related issues. One where you are again fit and healthy, doing the things you really want to do with your life.

Read through the list of areas to visualise given below, before you start your visualisation. Then, when you have them clear in your head, *see yourself*, in your mind's eye, as if through the lens of a camera, as you are in the future, doing the things you want to do, with all the ability, strength and energy to do them. Make the dream as rich and as bright as you can. Clearly see yourself as you would like to be. Give yourself the permission and the power to be whatever you dream of becoming. Have fun – make the dream a wonderfully compelling future!

Think about these areas, when you look to the future, and see them, as you would like them to be:

- **Health**   How do I want to be in a few years' time? Will losing weight improve my chances of survival? Will it enable me to enjoy many more healthy and active years? *See yourself with a clean bill of health, enjoying a long and happy older age, carefree, pain-free, without medication – all those health problems long gone.*

- **Fitness**   How agile, strong, flexible and toned will I be when I have completed this programme? *Look at how you will be. How do you see yourself in a few years, when all the weight has been lost and you are doing all the things you dreamed of? What things are you doing? How do you look doing them? How well can you do them? Picture yourself excelling at your favourite sport or physical activity.*

- **Social life**   How will this change? Will I be able to feel comfortable once more with my partner? Will I feel confident walking into business meetings and receptions? Will I feel at ease in my body? Will I feel comfortable going on the beach once more? *See yourself in all your social settings and feel how good it is to have this new body – the one you really want. Look at yourself as if through the lens of a camera and see yourself surrounded by others in all these social situations that you would want to be in, in the future. How do you look? How does that make you feel? What are you wearing? Have you got a special outfit with some amazing colours that you wouldn't dare to wear now? Have fun, you can wear whatever you want – nothing at all, if you prefer!*

- **Sport**   Can I win that club competition that has eluded me for so long? Will losing weight help me to do that? *See yourself achieve your sporting ambition. Clearly look at yourself as you go up to receive the award or prize. Think about how you won and what it felt like when you* *knew that you had done it. It was a magic moment in your life – how does that make you feel? What other sporting or athletic achievement would you enjoy? See yourself doing that – feel the pleasure you gain from it. Capture that sense of pride as you achieve your goal.*

*   **Energy**   Will losing weight give me more stamina and strength to do a better job? Will I have more energy for when I have time with family and friends?
    See yourself with all the energy you want to have. What are you doing? What can you do that you cannot do now? What are you capable of doing? How do you feel when you are doing these things? Picture yourself with so much vibrant energy that you could 'bounce off the walls'! How do you look and feel with so much energy inside you?

When your dream is bright and clear and you can see yourself as you will be in the future, capture it on paper.

Making it Real

To anchor the dream in reality, set some stepping stones along the way. You need to set a strategy to move you from where you are now, to where you see yourself in the future. You now have a brilliant vision of what the future will be, and you really want to hold on to that vision, making it as bright and as clear as possible. But you also need little achievements, mini peaks along the way. This is like building a mountain with grains of sand. After all, when is the future? The future starts in the next minute and goes on for as long as you can envisage your life lasting and that's why stepping stones are important in moving towards the building of that dream.

Now you are ready to write the second part of your Picture in Words, the stepping stones to take you to your dream. Then sign it and date it. If you want some more help, this is how it might look:

My dream is that in three years' time I will be running in and completing a marathon. My stepping stones to achieve that are:

- After one week I will have reduced my alcohol intake by 50 per cent. (Date . . .)
- Within one month I will be able to calculate the calories in most meals and I will have reduced my fat intake by 25 per cent. (Date . . .)
- In three months I will be walking for 10 miles (16km) without a problem and will have lost at least 1 stone (6.3kg) in weight. (Date . . .)
- Within a year I want to play golf again and to have the energy to keep up with my friends when we go skiing. (Date . . .)
- In 18 months I will have selected a personal trainer and agreed a programme that will enable me to run a marathon in 36 months from now. The marathon I have chosen to run in is . . . . (Date and location of the marathon . . .)

(Signed & dated)

I once had a dream that I would run a marathon – I have surpassed it by running more than one and competing in triathlons. As this book is being written I am training for the Great Bike Hike, which involves walking from John O'Groats to Land's End and then immediately cycling back. I am doing this to raise awareness, across Britain, of the work of the Family Heart Association. I achieved all this at over 50, having started to exercise in my late forties, never having done any long-distance running in my life. I mention these achievements, not because I wish to be seen as exceptional, nor because I want to impress you. What I want to emphasise and impress upon you, however, is that I'm not exceptional. It's only because I'm an average person who has managed to focus and train over a consistently long period of time, that I have been able to achieve these things, and that is all. It's by taking *tiny steps at a time*, that eventually, with perseverance and by celebrating your achievements along the way, you will get there. As my first marathon medal said: 'Success is a journey, not a destination.' For more on the Great Bike Hike and how to participate visit www.greatbikehike.co.uk.

Key points

- Complacency is the number one enemy, so keep your Picture in Words close at hand.

- Deep self-knowledge of why you want to succeed will support you to get there.

- Try for the first month to add at least one new reason a day for why you are doing this programme.

- Absolute honesty about your current situation will pay future dividends.

- Dream big, allow your wildest imagining to be at least a possibility.

- Put small, realistic and achievable stepping stones in place to bring the dream into reality.

7
Mind-set I

> ## Objectives
>
> - To develop the will to change
>
> - To discover how the change process works
>
> - To find out what may prevent it from working

Strong motivation and focus are vital to success, whether in business or your weight management programme. In this chapter you will learn about finding your own motivating factors and developing your personal focus, and will discover how to work with them to bring about change.

The first few days of a weight management programme are no different from the first few days of a new role at work or running a new project: you are spending your time learning new skills and working hard at change. If you are not sufficiently motivated the chances of success in either area are very limited.

Ask yourself why you picked up this book. Because you want to lose weight and get fitter? Well, that's fine because those are the specific areas we are going to work on, but there is one other area that will make the crucial difference to your success or failure and that is your mind-set. By mind-set I mean the way you look at things, the way you filter information through to your brain and the way it feels to you, and the way you interpret information that comes to you.

Remember – if you are to succeed as a Warrior, you need to change.

The Fundamental Elements That Lead to Change

As human beings we tend to resist change. If, however, you understand the process of change better, your chances of success will be infinitely improved. Business managers have long understood this, and there are many tried-and-tested theories around, advising on to how to cope with and manage change. The idea here is to look at a theory of change as it applies to a business and then use the same skills and knowledge in the management of your own body.

The formula I will use as an example here is the Change Equation, based on the work of Lewin and developed by management consultants, Sheppard Moscow. This diagram shows the accepted stages we move through when faced with change.

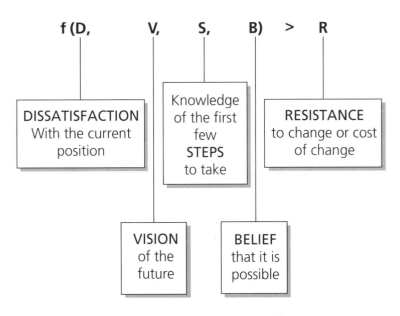

The Change Equation Formula

Take a close look at the four fundamental elements of change, as shown in the diagram:

- Dissatisfaction
- Vision
- Steps
- Belief

You need to be clear what your feelings are about all four elements, in order to ensure that you will be successful in your chosen objective – to change. In your notebook, or on your PC, list the above headings, each one on a separate page. Then, drawing on the work you did in your Business Plan in Chapter 5, and the Picture in Words in Chapter 6, you can now move on to analyse where you stand in relation to these areas. Below are some questions you can use to help you.

Dissatisfaction

- How deep is your dissatisfaction with where you are now?
- Can you describe it graphically?
- Can you really make it an imperative to change?

This way of thinking is a powerful tool – it is work you have already done in Chapter 6. The intention here is to recognise that you are genuinely and deeply dissatisfied with your present state, because that will inspire you to successful change.

Vision

How impelling is your vision of the future? Look again at your notes from Chapter 6 and distil from it the essence of what you want from your body; your new way of life; your dream of how you want your life to be and how you see your body serving you in the process. Make this bright and clear. Ensure that you have a future that you *really want* to move towards.

Steps

What steps do you need to take to move from where you are now to where you wish to be in the future (from dissatisfaction to vision)? Again, your work from Chapters 5 and 6 (Business Plan and Picture in Words) will provide you with all the necessary raw material. What is important is that you are totally clear about *how* you are going to do this and *when*.

Belief

You can spend lots of time planning, and you can take in all the theory that I can give you, through this Warriors programme, to build a compelling future but if there is no belief, then none of it will work. So you need to decide for yourself how realistic your plan and your vision are. Look at the SMART objectives that you set in your Business Plan. If you have really made them SMART (specific; measurable; achievable; *realistic* and time measurable), you are already most of the way to believing in what you are about to do. What I am asking you to do is *get committed.* Make up your mind that if you do all the things you plan to do – things that you know will work, and give it your best shot, then you will succeed – no question!

In business you do this all the time. If you did not believe in your business, it would be most unlikely to succeed. You, managing your body/business, are no different. You own it; believe in it and make it a success!

The Consequence Factor

We looked at 'consequences' in Chapter 5 (The Business Plan) and saw how, in business, there are immediate and obvious consequences when the business is badly run. We also saw how one of the most difficult areas in weight management to learn how to deal with is the fact that the consequences are gradual and the results are not immediate. You may think that one more pint, one sticky bun, one more canapé at a cocktail party, is not going to 'break the bank'. Indeed, none of these things will break the bank on their own. But it is those little grains of sand, those tiny morsels, that will build your body into something looking like a mountain!

The problem is in recognising the consequences at the time, so you need to decide how to introduce consequences for yourself. For instance, in the process of change, in the four areas you have just considered, the consequences of not having sufficient clarity or commitment in any one of those areas, will become apparent, over time. To see how it works, see page 113.

The table shows that if any of the ingredients for change is missing, the consequence will be failure, so for maximum success, remember the following pointers:

- If you have a sufficiently strong level of **dissatisfaction** and you can hold on to that for a long period of time, go back periodically to remind yourself of how you really felt at your lowest point.

- If you have a clear **vision** of how you see the future, and that vision is bright and compelling, that will pull you forward towards your goals.

- If you have identified the practical first **steps** and you have made those SMART, you will know precisely what you want to do from now until you reach your goals.

- If you really **believe** you can do it, because your Business Plan is sound and you have genuinely committed yourself, then when **resistance** to change occurs, as it inevitably will, you will be able to drive through it and you will succeed!

At the end of the day, you really have to want to do this. It can't be for anybody else – it's got to be for you.

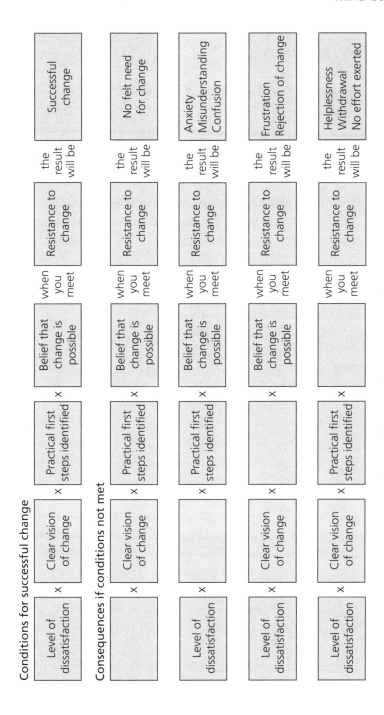

The conditions and consequences for change

Key points

- Be sure that you know your motivating factor for weight loss.

- To succeed, you must be genuinely willing to change.

- Be clear on where you are with the four essential factors in the Change Equation: dissatisfaction, vision, steps and belief.

8
Culture Change

Objectives

- To understand the different stages on the change curve

- To realise the importance of positive self-image

- To enlist the support and understanding of your partner

- To understand how to cope with resistance from family, friends and colleagues

If you want to re-shape your business and put it on a success-ful footing, understanding and using the concept of culture change is always necessary. Managing your body by imple-menting a weight management programme in the form of lifestyle changes requires an identical approach.

The Conditions for Successful Change

In business management the Kubler-Ross 'change curve' is often applied. This indicates typical responses to the need for change as they occur over time, from shock, denial, blaming others, blaming yourself, confusion and uncertainty, accep-tance and decision-making, to problem-solving and learning. I want to help you look at this change curve now from three different angles, as you think about your body/business. These are:

1. Yourself
2. Your wife, partner, or someone with whom you have an intimate relationship
3. People who are closest to you, such as close family members and friends.

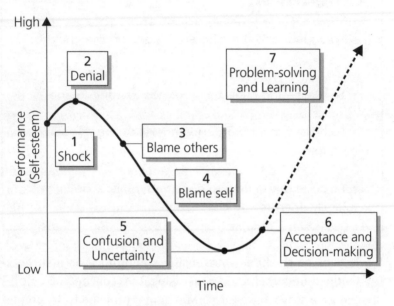

Change curve diagram

Culture Change: Yourself

Where do you stand, in relation to the change curve? Look at the various changes someone goes through in order to experience change and then apply them to your particular circumstances, as defined in your Business Plan.

1. Shock

First is the *shock*. Have you had a shock of some description related to your weight? If so, what was it? The results of a medical? Looking in the mirror? A comment from someone that you looked out of shape? Or are your joints starting to give you problems?

2. Denial

You may have gone through the *denial* stage by trying to convince yourself that it's not really that bad. When I weighed over 22 stone (140kg) I would challenge the doctors to give me something to work on. I needed something that said I had to lose weight. What I was really doing was not admitting to myself that I had a problem, which would only get worse, as time went on.

3. Blaming others

Then, having had a shock and gone into denial, you accept that things have gone wrong and you look for ways to *blame others*. In the case of weight management it's often looking at other diets you have tried that have failed – they let you down. Or you are sure that there is a magic cure but you have just not found it yet (this can also be part of denial). Or you may take to blaming your work. There is not enough time to eat a decent diet and exercise on a regular basis. All those business lunches and dinners! Or, you say that you have to go for a drink after work – it's a vital part of team building and networking with colleagues. Or, when you work from home there is always food around the house. Do any of these sound familiar to you?

4. Blaming self

Gradually you begin to realise that there is a problem; that it's not anyone else's fault but yours and you start to give yourself a really hard time – you *blame yourself*. You feel you have let yourself down and your self-confidence and your sense of self-worth start to take a hammering. As you do that, the problem gets worse. You seek the comfort of another drink or a good meal to cheer yourself up, and all the time the clothes are getting tighter and the problem is literally expanding.

5. Confusion

Finally you hit an all-time low. You begin to think that this weight problem has you stumped. *Confusion and uncertainty* set in, and you wonder what on earth you can do. There is nowhere to go because all those diet self-help groups are female-biased. Besides, you would rather die than admit that you have a problem to the world at large. You no longer know the difference between a good diet and a bad diet; all the messages you have been getting are so contradictory. High protein and high fat? Or low fat and no carbohydrates? The list goes on and on.

6. Acceptance and decision making

And then one bright day you were browsing in a bookshop and came out with *Warriors*. You realise that there is an issue, and that it can be resolved by building your own strategy and conquering this demon. This is the stage of *acceptance and decision making*, where your problem-solving skills start to lock in and your performance improves. You start to lose weight and gain energy, and all of a sudden your self-confidence is back again. This is the way life should be – rich and enjoyable. You're on a roll and change has occurred successfully.

Where Are You Now?

Is the foregoing a process that you can relate to? Where are you on the change curve right now? If you don't think you've reached the *acceptance and decision making* stage yet, go back and review your Picture in Words from Chapter 6. Look at your Business Plan too and try to see if there is something missing, something that will move you along the curve towards change.

If you are currently overweight, then certain established habits and conditions enabled you to achieve that result. Clearly you want to change, otherwise you would be unlikely to have read this far. That being the case, what are some of the habits or patterns that will need to change, in order for you to achieve the successful outcome you seek? Fairly obviously, the most important are nutrition and exercise.

Nutrition

As we saw in Chapter 3, watch the quality, quantity and frequency of your input. Ensure that you have sufficient for your needs – that means *adequate* calories, *balanced* over a range of foods. Remember that anything that falls outside the definitions of adequate and balanced relates to emotional eating and can be put down to boredom, habit or stress. When you find that change has not occurred and you are still repeating the old patterns, become a detective with your food. Learn how to solve the riddle of your eating patterns by slotting them into one of the three brackets (boredom, habit or stress) and then work on the solution. That means looking for ways to break the patterns in the future so that you can ensure you stick with your chosen course. You do that by recording the 'events' in your mood diary. These may be new habits, which need to be repeated sufficiently often (21 repetitions are required to establish a new habit) to make sure they become ingrained.

Exercise

Allocating sufficient time for exercise and working at the ideal intensity, as defined in Chapter 4, is all that is necessary.

Your Attitude

If it's that easy to manage your weight, why can't we all do it?

Because the practice is harder than you think. The key, therefore, is the mind-set – your attitude. That is a tough area to crack and this book has looked at many of the ways you can do that, but no one can will you to do this – not even you. You have to *want* to do it. Once you *really* want to do it, it becomes much easier. It is that culture change inside you that is so important. You have to feel you are worth the effort and that the effort carries sufficient rewards. You also need to feel that there are sufficient consequences, which would be unacceptable, if you remained the way you are right now. If you can do that then the process will be easier too.

Self-image

A really important point to consider, when you deal with your own culture change, is how you see yourself. Think about your own self-image now. Do you see yourself as one of the lads when it comes to drinking – able to hold your own with the best? Or do you see yourself as a bit of a foodie – someone who can talk knowledgeably about the best restaurants in town and the best wines on their menus? Do you see yourself as someone who is big, strong and powerful, because you can literally throw your weight around, if you want to? Think about how you see yourself and the image that comes to your mind.

Now, relate your current self-image to the one you see in the future – the one you saw when you did the visualisation exercise for your Picture in Words in Chapter 6. Did you see a fit, healthy executive in designer clothes? A happy, energetic dad with his kids? A lean and mean troubleshooter?

Is that fit and healthy image one that is congruent with your current identity? If not, how do they differ? What is it about your present image that may be contributing to your present excess weight? Work on how you want to see yourself in the future and try to match that to reality today. In other words, start already behaving and acting as if you were that person in the future.

> Remember, your image on the inside always becomes your image on the outside.

I had a self-image of Henry VIII from a very young age, because it made me feel stronger and more powerful, when inside I was feeling weak and unrecognised. As I gradually lived out that image I became more and more like my early hero – including the size of my girth.

Becoming a Warrior

When thinking about your own culture change, consider developing some of the best qualities of the Warrior within yourself. Think of a man who is both mentally and physically strong, a man of his word, who has integrity with himself and the world at large, who commits to a course of action and sees it through to the end, who is proud of who he is and what he does, and who commands respect because of who he is and what he has become. These are all rich qualities. They will give you considerable strength as you start to manage your body.

Look for these special qualities in other men and benchmark against them. Choose the areas where you would like to be stronger and find people who have those qualities so they can act as your guide or role model. To start you off, think of the spirit of adventure of Richard Branson, the compassion of the Dalai Lama or the nobility of Nelson Mandela.

Culture Change: Your Partner

Your weight-loss programme will inevitably affect your wife or partner, or whoever plays this role in your life, too, and it is as important, as it is respectful, to give them the opportunity to share parts of it with you. Fundamental to that will be your ability to communicate with each other. For you, the would-be Warrior, think about the following:

- What do you want from your partner?
- How can they help you?
- Are there any things that they can do that would make the process easier?

Ask your partner to address the following issues:

- What are the best ways to help my partner manage their weight?
- What are the issues they will face?
- How can you encourage them?

You – vis-à-vis your partner

If, hypothetically, you could have the best person in the world supporting you with your weight management programme, who and what would they be?

- Write down all the qualities you would value from this person and what they would be doing to support you.

- Write down a list of all the things you would want from that person.

- Think about the things that have been most damaging in relation to your partner's attitude towards your weight.

- What would you like to tell your partner in relation to your weight? Would you be prepared to tell them how you really feel? Would you consider sharing parts of your Picture in Words with them?

When you have a clear idea of how you would like to be supported in your programme and what, so far, has been unhelpful behaviour from your partner, you are in a position to discuss matters with them. Your next step is to think about how best to put it across.

This can be a very difficult area for some people – especially for men. We do not like sharing our innermost feelings with others. We hate feeling vulnerable and we especially loathe being supported. These are all things which men tend to spurn. After all, our origins are as Warrior hunter-gatherers. Men had to be strong and courageous, to defend our women and children from attack and to hunt for food, often risking our own lives in the process. We needed to be able to control our emotions, to keep our heads in the heat of battle, not to flee when attacked by a wild animal but to stand our ground and fight back. And to do that we had to suppress many of our basic and natural instincts as human beings. Although very few of us are faced with those physically life-threatening situations today, these 'qualities' of strength and silence are still there, although they serve very little purpose in our lives.

So consider some change, so that you get what you really want. Women love to talk, to share feelings – to communicate. If you are prepared to open up and expose your vulnerability to a woman who *genuinely loves you*, she will feel valued and trusted, and will do all in her power to reciprocate. She may be a little bowled over initially, as this could well be out of character for you – but go gently with her, because when she realises what is happening she will value you and the relationship far more. She will serve as a very powerful ally in helping you on the road to success. Do not underestimate the benefits of this.

If you are still unsure about opening up, and telling your partner what you want, then think about this:

- How did you feel when you went for your first job interview? Did you feel vulnerable then? How did you overcome those fears? Was it through good preparation and anticipation of what was about to come? If you have those skills you can use them here too.

- How did you feel when you first started to go out with your partner – the first time you became intimate? Did you feel vulnerable on those occasions? How did you handle the situation at that time? Apply those skills to the present situation. After all, you are only telling her what you really want! You deserve no less, in a good and loving relationship.

Your partner – vis-à-vis you

This next section is aimed at your partner – let them read it, if you wish.

By the time you read this, your partner may have already discussed the Warriors programme with you. If so, that is a great advantage. But if not, read on anyway because this is designed to give your partner the best chance possible to succeed in his weight management programme. Your support and understanding will be of great benefit and my purpose here is to give you some tips as to how this can be done to best effect.

First, ask yourself, honestly, if you are prepared to really help your partner. Perhaps your answer will surprise you. Have you considered any of the following circumstances:

- Do you feel threatened by what may happen, if your partner suddenly becomes fit and active?

- Are you afraid of changes that may occur as a result of your partner losing weight and therefore becoming more attractive?

In the short term it may be hard for you. Your partner may become irritable and despondent. He will be fighting a battle and it will not always be easy. On some occasions he will be confronting himself. He will need support and encouragement when that happens. In the long run he will become a better and more fulfilled person – one who understands himself and what he wants out of life, far better than he may do today. To that extent he will face up to some real issues in his life, and as he challenges and overcomes those his morale will improve – as will his confidence and self-esteem.

It may be a delicate question, but have you ever teased or criticised your partner about how he looks? Have you ever tried to get your partner to lose weight and change his ways by pointing out his defects? So often men who are over-weight know what it is doing to them and the risks they are running – but until they are ready to change (and that change has to come from within) all that anyone else may say or do will only serve to make matters worse. Go easy on him. It is true that bullying can sometimes bring about a temporary change as he goes on a crash diet, but Warriors is not about temporary change, it is about ensuring that the weight comes off, and stays off for good!

Motivational support

In practice, of course, none of us is perfect. Your partner will, from time to time, be unable to stick rigidly to the pro-gramme. There will be times when he will want to eat things that are either too high in calories, outside his meal plan or outside the hours he planned to eat. If he chooses to do that, accept that it is his choice. Something else will be going on that is more powerful than he can handle at that stage. If you criticise or bully him at that point he will feel ten times worse and is much less likely to stick with the programme than if you leave him to his own devices. When he deviates from the programme he will already feel bad about it, even if he does not let it show. See if he might want to talk about what is causing him to eat in that way. It could well be relat-ed to one of three main areas:

- habit
- boredom or
- stress.

It is possible he is tired or in pain, and is using food to pro-vide a temporary energy boost or as a form of consolation Whatever it is, you will almost certainly be able to help him

– if you can find the way to show you really care and want to give him that support. If you know what is at the root of it, see if you can do something which may distract him long enough to get away from the situation, so he can refocus and remind himself of the important goals he is committed to in the Warriors programme.

Some questions for partners of would-be Warriors

- Do you know why your partner wants to lose weight?

- Have you asked him whether he has any goals, set within the Warriors programme, that he may wish to share with you?

- If you do most of the cooking, are you prepared to rearrange your kitchen and eating habits to accommodate what your partner will need, in order to succeed with his diet?

- Are you prepared for the fact that you may not be able to have as many rich or calorific meals as perhaps you have had in the past?

- What form of exercise would be enjoyable for you to do together?

- Are you prepared for your partner to be grumpy sometimes – because he is fighting a tough battle with himself?

Practical support

There are two key areas that will be important to the success of the programme: nutrition and exercise (but of course your partner's state of mind is crucial, too).

1. **Nutrition** He needs to eat the right amount of calories per day – no more, no less. He needs to plan ahead so that he can keep tabs on how he is doing, both in terms of quality and quantity, as well as time and location for eating. And he needs plenty of variety in his food, with nothing ruled out, not even fat. The guiding principle is the energy consumption. If you tend to do most of the cooking and shopping in your household, have a look at Chapter 3 of this book, where nutritional guidelines are spelt out.

2. **Exercise** He needs to do at least three aerobic exercise sessions per week of half-an-hour or more. That does not necessarily mean pumping iron at the gym – a brisk walk may, at the outset, be sufficient. It helps if some of that activity is shared with others, so you could go dancing, walking, cycling or perhaps play golf or tennis together.

It really is that simple! If he sticks to this faithfully, over a sufficiently long period, his weight will come down and he will be able to keep it at that lower level.

Your rewards

- A healthier and fitter partner who has more energy to share the things that you really enjoy doing.

- A partner who stands a good chance of living a far longer life, with a better quality of life in older age.

- A partner who is far less prone to illness.

> • A man with greater self-esteem and self-respect,
> which will enhance your relationship as he starts to
> live life in greater harmony with himself.

Culture change: family, friends and colleagues

Friends and family can sometimes be the worst offenders
when it comes to 'support'. They often mean well, but they
tend to have strong habits that have been built up over a
lifetime and any change can leave them feeling threatened
or vulnerable.

Be aware of these sentiments and allay their fears. Explain
to them that this is something you really want to do and that it
is vital that you do it to the best of your ability – because it will,
without doubt, improve your health and your life expectancy.
Do not let them literally kill you with their kindness. Point this
out to them gently. They may need reassurance that you will
still care about them and you will still value them, even if you
do not have second helpings of everything that is offered!

Drinking 'buddies', whether work colleagues or old friends,
can pose a real problem. This is culture change at one of its
deepest levels for some men. As I found when I undertook my
own weight-loss programme, real buddies are real buddies and
it does not matter to them whether you are drinking or not. If
they can see that this is really important to you and that you
need to do it for your health and general well-being, then they
will respect you all the more and hopefully give you very little
grief about it. It is often those with the greatest insecurities who
shout the loudest. They don't like the idea that someone near
them is 'shaping up'. This can make them feel uncomfortable
and they will do everything they can to get you back to their
bad habits. Frankly, such people are hardly real buddies.

Key points

- Managing culture change is something you already know about at work, so just apply it to your weight management programme.

- Identify the different points on the change curve, and know where you are now.

- It takes 21 repetitions to change a habit, so start now.

- Don't underestimate how difficult it can be to change established patterns.

- Identify whether you break your new healthy eating and exercise routines out of boredom, habit or stress, and make the necessary change.

- Remember, your body image on the inside is invariably the one reflected on the body outside, so make yours as positive as possible.

- Enlist the help of your partner, family and friends – their support will make all the difference.

9
Time Management

Objectives

- To implement your Business Plan

- To learn to schedule your priorities

- To set up a system for time planning on a daily, weekly and monthly basis

- To see how to put the Warriors programme into effect on a very tight schedule

As with business management, one of the keys to successful weight management is how willing you are to properly allocate dedicated time to establishing, running and maintaining your programme. You will need to concentrate on the following areas:

- training
- nutrition
- planning and review.

The important issues here are knowing how much time you need to allocate to each area and above all, how to stick with your time commitments. These are a vital part of a successful outcome.

By the end of this chapter you should have decided how much time you need to allocate to run your body/business and where that time will come from. If you find that the overall time is short, then you will need to establish where you will delegate further. You may also decide that greater efficiency is your best option, so look again at what you are trying to do and decide if you can do it better. Perhaps you could think about taking exercise in the morning to avoid having to shower and change twice in the day, or if you don't want to miss out on your social life, take up sports that involve your family and friends, so that you can be with them, while at the same time fulfilling your need for exercise.

If you do decide, after a thorough review, that you cannot fit everything in and that you have no better option than to compromise – accept that each compromise has its own consequences (less exercise means slower loss of excess weight). Ensure that the decisions you make take those consequences into account.

The Concept of Priorities

Stephen Covey, in his book *First Things First*, tells a story that illustrates the importance of not prioritising your schedule, but scheduling your priorities.

I attended a seminar once where the instructor was lecturing on time. At one point, he said, 'Okay, it's time for a quiz.' He reached under the table and pulled out a wide-mouth gallon jar. He set it on the table next to a platter with some fist-sized rocks on it. 'How many of these rocks do you think we can get in the jar?' he asked.

After we made our guess, he said, 'Okay. Let's find out.' He set one rock in the jar ... then another ... then another. I don't remember how many he got in, but he got the jar full. Then he asked, 'Is that jar full?'

Everybody looked at the rocks and said, 'Yes'.

Then he said, 'Ahhh.' He reached under the table and pulled out a bucket of gravel. Then he dumped some gravel in and shook the jar and the gravel went in all the little spaces left by the big rocks. Then he grinned and said once more, 'Is the jar full?'

By this time we were on to him. 'Probably not,' we said.

'Good!' he replied. And he reached under the table and brought out a bucket of sand. He started dumping the sand in and it went in all the little spaces left by the rocks and the gravel. Once more he looked at us and said, 'Is the jar full?'

'No!' we all roared.

He said, 'Good!' and he grabbed a pitcher of water and began to pour it in. He got something like a quart of water in that jar. Then he said, 'Well, what's the point?'

Somebody said, 'Well, there are gaps, and if you really work at it, you can always fit more into your life.'

'No,' he said, 'that's not the point. The point is this: if you hadn't put these big rocks in first, would you ever have gotten any of them in?'

Covey goes on to say:

With the 'more is better' paradigm, we're always trying to fit more activities into the time we have. But what does it matter how much we do if what we're doing isn't what matters most?

This story applies equally well to the important things you intend to do, in this Warriors programme. Remember, the rocks are your priorities; they need to be put in first. The gravel, sand and water are all the other things that fill the rest of your time. They can be adjusted, 'settled', once the priorities are in place. It's about getting the important things in and focusing on them so that in terms of time management, you give them priority, otherwise there is a good chance that they will never get in at all!

The Importance of Planning

All managers know that efficiency in time management is absolutely essential to a successful business. Similarly, when thinking about your body/business, you will need to cover all aspects of how you are going to plan your time on a daily, weekly and monthly basis. Time expended in planning definitely comes back as rich rewards later, but at the outset it's rather like the rocket launch. You see it lift off a few feet from the ground – which doesn't seem like much progress – yet huge amounts of fuel and energy have gone into just those first few seconds. It's the same with your Warriors programme – you need to spend time and energy getting the system into place. You are now running a new business – extra time to get it into shape, especially at the beginning, is vital if it is to succeed.

> To attempt the Warriors Programme without an adequate time management structure in place is to embark upon a route that will lead to failure.

I offer suggestions in this chapter, based on what has worked for me, but you need to fathom out what time management system works best for you, because you are the one who has to live with it! It's not possible to tell you what you must do and when, such as 'every morning you must get up and write your diary' or something similar. It's up to you to find out what suits you.

Your system does not need to be highly sophisticated. It must, however, identify how you will guarantee to spend sufficient time on your exercise, nutrition, and planning and review.

Again, we can look at the same principles applied here as in any other business, as in the following table:

Any business	Your body/business
Production	Exercise
Raw materials and energy supplies	Nutrition
Vision for the future, and ongoing monitoring of progress and results	Ensuring you get what you want from your body, now and in the future

Long-term forward planning

A strong, clear boost of effort at the outset is important. If you can, it would be a really good idea to take some time out of work – a couple of days' holiday, or a long weekend, to start developing your vision for your body/business (see pages 101–7 for details of how to undertake this). It will include your Business Plan (from Chapter 5) and your Picture in Words (from Chapter 6). Make this the time that you really focus on everything that you want to do and begin to understand the new company you are about to manage – your body. There is a Zen quotation that illustrates this point perfectly: 'He who plans in the temple wins the war'. In other words, it's not in the heat of the battle that you make the most informed choices; it's in the 'temple' of the initial planning stage that you find out all the factors that will make the difference between success and failure. I called this programme Warriors because I could see an inner battle taking place and, like a Warrior, you aspire to be mentally strong and physically fit. That requires the devotion of time, effort and considerable thought to what you are doing, before you even start the programme.

Setting the ball rolling

When you have completed the initial planning of your priorities, you can start to look at what time element is actually going to be involved in this new way of life and how you are going to build it in to your current lifestyle.

Of course the main time management tool is the allocation of time itself. You will need three things to hand, in whatever form you like, in order to do this:

- your day-to-day diary with defined time segments throughout the day
- your Food and Mood diary (see Chapter 3)
- an exercise log (see Chapter 4).

To save time, you can order the Warriors start-up pack, which includes these items (see Useful Addresses, page 186).

The basics

At the start of each week you are going to sit down and slot in times in your business diary for food management, leisure and exercise. Go through the following checklist with your diary:

- **External structure** You need to work with your business commitments, so the first thing to do is look at any areas of potential conflict. For example, if you have two breakfast meetings set up, is it still feasible to have your run beforehand or are you going to have to move it to another slot?

- **Exercise** Block in your regular exercise time next. What type of exercise are you planning? How much time do you need to allocate?

- **Nutrition** Block in time for food planning, shopping, preparation time and cooking (if you're responsible for that).

- **Time off** Last but not least, put in your leisure pursuits. If you don't plan for them, they won't happen and you need a balance of work and play. Build in time for some pleasurable activities to 'reward' yourself for sticking with the programme, or just to make yourself feel better if you are having a tough week.

Here is an example of a typical couple of days' diary, of someone at the beginning of a Warriors Programme. The priority activities are in bold type:

	Monday	Tuesday	Wednesday	Thursday	Friday	Saturday	Sunday
7.00	*Run*	*Breakfast*	*Run*		*Bike*		
7.30	*Shower*	*Travel*					
8.00	*Breakfast*	*Airport*					
8.30	*Travel*	*Meetings*				*Run*	
9.00 to	*Work*						
1.00	*Lunch*	*Lunch at desk*					
2.00 to	*Work*	*Work*					
5.30	*Travel*						
6.00	*Travel*	*Bike*					
6.30	*Cook*	*Shower*					
7.00	*Cook*	*Cinema*		*Swim*	*Theatre*		
7.30							
8.00	*Eat*			*Cook*			
8.30	*Relax at home*						
9.00		*Eat dinner*					
9.30	*Bath/bed*						

Time allocated to priorities: training, food preparation, leisure, exercise

Flexible Time Management

You are planning for the best way to incorporate your new routine into your daily life. This also means allowing yourself flexibility when you need to change something, but without letting yourself off the hook. It's the reality of comparing and balancing, and asking, what are my priorities, what is more important? So, you plan to go to the gym but you also have a last-minute marketing report to produce. Now you are also running this new business, your body/business, and even though it's not paying you a salary or financial dividends you are still looking for a good return on the time and energy you have expended. What is your priority? Can you find time to go to the gym or not? If you decide not to go, you want to be very clear about the basis of your decision, and the consequences of making that decision.

Flexible time management in the key areas

- Always allow time for writing up your diaries and logs. Remember, these are essential monitoring tools.

- If you are a morning person, exercising first thing sets you up for the day and means you can then forget about it.

- Compile shopping lists and plan menus simultaneously, to save time and to stop you from being sidetracked in supermarkets.

- If time is very scarce, get your shopping delivered (see Useful Addresses page 186 for a service aimed at reducing the need to menu plan, shop and count calories).

- Batch cook and freeze measured portions of healthy meals.

- Build in time to get feedback from your coaches and trainers.

- Do you need to work in a 'time budget' for training (for a weekend healthy cookery course or a basic martial arts course)?

Establishing Priorities

Begin to establish your priorities in time management by considering the areas that require the most time, and those are probably exercise and nutrition.

Exercise scheduling

After reading Chapter 4 of this book, you know at what level you are going to exercise, and how much you want to do in order to achieve your goals and objectives. That is what you need to build around. Maybe you've decided on aerobics three times a week, or a run every day, but whatever it is, you will need to programme that time, as well as establish the right time of day, for you. Be clear about the allocation of your time for these activities – it is an absolute pre-requisite for a fit and healthy body.

In addition to the time you require for exercising, you also will be completing your exercise log, as discussed in Chapter 4. This takes literally a few minutes at the time, as you will want to make some quick notes for when you are reviewing your progress. Remember, you are not writing an essay!

Nutrition

You have to spend time planning what you are going to eat, what to buy and how to cook it. By now you will have cleared your kitchen of temptation, and bought some equipment for your new lifestyle – such as a wok, a steamer and a microwave, and a range of useful low-fat, low-calorie cookbooks (see Further Reading page 195, for some good examples).

You may find it will be very time consuming at the outset, to plan menus and work out what foods you are going to eat that are healthy, nutritious and within your calorie budget. Plan ahead with your menus and block in the time needed for shopping, food preparation and cooking.

Always shop with a list of the items you intend to buy. This gives you purpose and will divert you from temptation. To optimise time planning, write out your shopping list at the same time as you do your menu planning. A further tip is to shop when you have just eaten – that makes the food on the shelves far less tempting. If you have to 'grab' a quick meal on the way home, make sure you know *exactly* what you want and don't be tempted to browse the shelves for ideas – you'll be hungry and sure to add some of the poorer choices to your basket – avoid doing that at all costs!

If time is at a real premium for you, cut out the shopping altogether and have home deliveries arranged (this reduces the possibilities for temptation even further).

Cooking is a critical area for time management. You've got to decide when you're going to cook, and how much you're going to do. It may be something that you really enjoy, in which case you can treat it like a hobby. It's possible your partner may be happy to support you by doing the cooking. Or you can use ready prepared healthy, low-calorie, low-fat meals.

A good way to save time in food preparation is to plan well ahead and cook meals in batches to freeze. If you are not into batch cooking, there are still plenty of time-saving options, such as stir-fry prawns and vegetables with rice – it's quicker than a takeaway and far lower in calories!

A final time management consideration on nutrition is to make sure you plan the time when you eat and preferably the location too. This is important, because if you permit yourself to eat at any time of day, and only record the calories you have consumed, several problems may arise:

1. You lay yourself open to temptation. If you know that you will only eat what you planned, and only eat it at the time you planned to do so, your chances of sticking with your programme are substantially greater. If you then come unstuck (which will happen) by eating something, which you had not planned, or eating something outside the time at which you planned to eat it, that serves as an excellent source of information. Record it in the Mood part of your food diary to help with your analysis at the end of the month. With that, you can build on improving your overall chances of success.

2. If you eat without a plan and at any time of day, the chances are you will eat when you are at your hungriest. That always leads to eating less appropriate foods, and often to bigger portion sizes.

3. By setting the places where you will eat, such as in the dining-room or always sitting at a table, you develop discipline and build up your mental strength, re-enforcing your ability to stick with the programme.

4. Take a few seconds to reflect before you eat. That brings you into the present and enables you to be really aware of what you are eating. Traditional families and those who are religious often say grace – that has the same effect and concentrates the mind on the present and the act of eating, rather than the distraction of watching television while having a meal. The point is, the more focused you are about what you are doing with food when you eat, the better your chances of success.

Checking with your team

Another time factor to budget for is measuring, assessing and getting appraisal from your team. Factor in the required time for feedback from your personal trainer, nutritionist and mindset coach if you engage them. Will you do it weekly, monthly, in person, or by phone or e-mail?

Time for training

This is not your physical training schedule, but the sort of additional skills or knowledge that you may be in need of to run this new body/business effectively. What sort of training do you want as a manager in your new business? Do you need extra culinary skills or do you need to know more about nutrition?

As a manager, if you never get input from new contacts and ideas, how soon is it before you are going to be outdated in your thinking? Wouldn't your body/business fare better if you take time out for some training? Perhaps joining one of the Warriors programmes would be something you may wish to consider? (Visit the Warriors website, see page 186, for further details.)

Planning for pleasure
One of the aims of the Warriors programme is to improve your health and fitness to enable you to do the things that you really enjoy. Whatever you enjoy, you need to consider what time you're going to be building in to your time management programme for it.

My solution to finding time for things I enjoy is to say that on an odd-numbered week, from the fifty-two weeks of the year, I would make time to go to the cinema and on an even-numbered week I would go to the theatre. By doing that, I knew I would fit it into my schedule, because I've focused on it and allowed time for it. If it didn't happen, as a result of business or other pressures, that was all right because the opportunity would come round again. These are not top priorities, like exercise and nutrition, so you can afford to be more flexible. They are perhaps the gravel in Stephen Covey's example earlier, rather than the rocks, but remember that leisure and fun time are important to your overall health and well-being.

Monitoring and Reviewing
The best way to measure your progress is to break it down into three critical steps:

* recording daily
* reviewing weekly
* analysing monthly.

These time scales are really important to the success of your programme:

- On a daily basis you're not trying to discover whether or not the business is working properly – all you're doing is recording what's going on.

- On a weekly basis, you're just reviewing that everything is going in the right direction.

- On a monthly basis, you are sitting down and asking if it's all really worthwhile. Stand back and really look at your body/business. Ask if it's getting you where you really want to go. This is where most of your review time is spent, on analysing what has happened during the month.

Daily recording

Of what you have eaten and where you ate outside your plan. If you are tracking your weight, you might want to weigh yourself every day. You certainly want to record your food intake on a daily basis to see how it has matched up against your plans, and you want to take a note of what training you did and how it went, each time you exercise.

Weekly review

On a weekly basis you should be reviewing your Food and Mood diary (see Chapter 3) and your exercise log (see Chapter 4). This will take you about half-an-hour. Note any patterns that are starting to build through the week. Look at your moods and see whether you can detect any relationships between events and, say, binge eating or training missed.

Your Food and Mood diary (see Chapter 3)

These are your weekly review questions:

- Did I meet my targets?
- Did I eat the planned amounts?

- Did I eat at the planned times?
- Did I eat what I planned to eat?
- Is my weight going in the right direction and at the right speed?
- If I ate outside the plan, was this due to stress, boredom or habit?
- What can I do to correct or improve my performance?

Your training log (see Chapter 4)

These records relate to your exercise programme. Here are your weekly review questions:

- Am I on target?
- Is my training where I want it to be?
- Do I need to adjust my programme content or intensity?
- Is there anything I need to discuss with my trainer?

Monthly analysis

Allow an hour for your monthly review. Sit back and have a good look at the last four weeks and see any patterns that may be starting to emerge, and how you're doing against your goals and objectives. Do you need to make any adjustments to your schedule? Here are some questions to consider:

- Did I meet my monthly goals?
- If not, what put me off?
- How can I now compensate to get me back on track?
- What really doesn't work and needs to be changed?

If you are on track, and have achieved your goal(s) for the month, give yourself *recognition* and a *bonus* or reward, just as you would a successful member of staff, in your business.

Then, plan for the month ahead. Are you currently on or off-track? Look at your Business Plan and decide what you need to do to ensure that you remain on track or what you require to do, to get back on track.

Correcting the course

If your analysis has shown that you are not on course, then you need to decide how you would move ahead faster. Take time out, and reflect on what you can do about it. For example, if you feel that you're not losing weight fast enough, that's an obvious one because your stock level is still too high and you want to get these stock levels down. These are some questions you could ask yourself about that:

- Am I still taking in too many calories?
- Are my portion sizes too big?
- Am I not taking enough exercise?
- Could it be that I haven't found enough ways of getting the exercise that I need?
- Is the weight moving more slowly just because my body takes time, perhaps longer than I thought it did?

Implementing the Warriors Programme

Below you will find suggestions for how to implement the Warriors programme from scratch in a relatively short time frame and yet maintain your sanity! So, let's get going.

Structure your time

1. Set a week aside for getting the programme going.

2. Spend Monday to Thursday giving *Warriors* a first reading.

3. Schedule Friday as a one-day holiday.

4. Arrange a medical for Friday – see Useful Addresses (see pages 188 and 191) for suggestions. You will be clearly guided by your doctor, but below are some areas that you need to cover:
   - Prostate for any signs of enlargement or possibility of cancer
   - Testes for the same reason
   - Blood pressure

- Heart rate and an electro-cardiogram (ECG)
- Cholesterol level
- Blood sugar
- Liver function.

6. Book a fitness test for Friday too – your local gym should be able to arrange this. This is what you want to know:
   - VO2 Max. This is your ability to use oxygen under exercise conditions.
   - Heart rate and how to find the right zone for exercise (see Chapter 4)
   - Strength
   - Flexibility
   - Endurance.

The last three are to assess the areas you may wish to improve.

Action day-by-day

Monday to Thursday

1. Read the book to get a good overview. You do not need to take notes in depth at this stage, but it will be useful to start forming some early ideas. Let your subconscious work on telling your system what it really wants.

2. On Monday book a medical and a fitness test for Friday. Go to a bookshop, or visit an on-line site to look at low-calorie cookbooks and choose a couple that interest you. (See Further Reading)

3. Decide, before Wednesday, whether you want to order a Warriors Kit so that it can be delivered in time for Thursday evening, when you will want to have the Food and Mood diary ready for action.

Thursday Evening

1. Read and work through Chapter 3 step-by-step. By the end of your reading you will:

   - Know how many calories you need per day.

   - Have your menu plan prepared for next week. The important thing here is to work through the menu plan and from that the meals you can make from it.

   - What you are trying to do is make enough food for your main meals of the week during the weekend. That way you will have very little cooking to do for the rest of the week. Remember to keep two out of three meals simple, and one more substantial. That way you do not have to spend your whole life in the kitchen!

   - Based on the food plan, you will have a shopping list.

   - Do you want to engage a dietitian (see Useful Addresses, page 186 for details)? Make sure you know what questions you want to ask and how you want to use their services.

2. Read Chapter 4 on exercise and work through it, step-by-step. Once you have done that you will:

   - Know what exercise you want to do, when, and how much.

   - Decide if you need any new kit such as a heart rate monitor, new trainers, Dynaband or shorts. Make out a shopping list.

- Decide whether you want to take on the services of a personal trainer and mind-set coach (see Useful Addresses, page 186). If so, make out a checklist of questions you want to ask before you meet or phone them.

- Decide if you want to join a gym or a club, and plan to visit a few on Friday.

3. From the information on pages 90–1 of Chapter 5, decide if you need any new kitchen equipment. By the end of Thursday evening you should be armed with the following:
   - Shopping lists for food, sports equipment and kitchenware.

   - Names and details, as well as checklists of questions for your dietitian, personal trainer and mind-set coach if you are planning to use them.

   - Name and details of sports clubs or gyms you are considering joining – ready for your market research tomorrow (Friday).

Friday

During the day, you should complete the following:
- Your medical

- Your fitness assessment

- Shopping for food, sports equipment and kitchenware

- Market research: dietitian, personal trainer and gym or sports club, mind-set coach.

In the evening:
- work through and complete Chapter 6 A Picture in Words

- read, but do not do, Chapter 5, and the earlier part of this chapter, to prepare your mind for tomorrow (Saturday).

Saturday
- First, read again your Picture in Words from yesterday evening. Fix it in your mind.

- Work through Chapter 5: Business Plan II. Do this section-by-section, but leave the 'Executive Summary' and 'Mission Statement' until tomorrow (Sunday). The reason for leaving these two documents for now is to give you a chance to reflect. These final two sections are designed to summarise your Business Plan and encapsulate your purpose, respectively. It is better to do that when you have had some distance from the subject and can therefore gain perspective.

- Allow at least three hours in the day to get in some cooking. You may be good at this or it may be your first time. Nowadays cooking is very 'sexy', with male chefs like Gary Rhodes, Rick Stein and Jamie Oliver as role models, and more and more men are finding it a relaxing and enjoyable pastime. Choose some dishes to make from your menu plan (see page 44) and get stock into the freezer to save you time later on.

- Enjoy Saturday night – relax! You deserve it. Give yourself some reward for getting this far. Choose a non-edible treat – get out, go to the cinema or theatre.

Sunday

- Finish your planning by completing the Executive Summary of the Business Plan and your Mission Statement in Chapter 5.

- Then, cook two more recipes and freeze them for next week.

- Finally, settle back and re-read Chapter 8 and Chapters 10–12. These should motivate you and let you see how to face life in the real world when you go back to work on Monday.

Key points

- The main areas you need to consider when planning your time are nutrition, exercise, and planning and review.

- Record daily, review weekly, analyse monthly.

- Define your priorities and fit them in first.

- Clear planning at the outset is vital.

- Every week, slot into the external structure of your diary (your work and social commitments) the internal structure of your Warriors programme.

- Planning must incorporate some flexibility, but compromise will always have consequences.

- The week spent implementing your Business Plan will reap dividends many times over.

10
Handling External Pressures

Objectives

- To plan for travel and eating out

- To understand how to handle business and social situations where suitable food isn't on offer

- To learn how to keep up your exercise routine when away from home

When travelling and eating out you have less control over the outside world, and it is there that you can face your greatest challenge. A business analogy is opening up new offices or regional branches. When you travel away from home, on trips abroad, it's like running an overseas subsidiary. You need to adapt to local conditions, speak a new language and acclimatise to different cultures. You have to adjust to the fact that running your body/business when you go out, or travel abroad, is little different. You are still running the business with the core values of the company. Your objectives have not changed – but the turf has! You have to adapt to local conditions, but retain your focus. In this chapter you will find strategies to use when faced with everyday situations that could challenge your Warriors Programme.

Eating Out

There are, broadly, three categories your eating out will fit into:

- business
- social
- special occasions and celebrations.

They all have different potential pitfalls. The best way to tackle them is with forward planning, where you have enough notice, or with skilful menu strategy, where you don't. In either case, you will be helped by having a positive attitude.

Working Lunches

These can sometimes be awkward. If it is unplanned, and you are just carrying on from a meeting that has gone on longer than expected, there's often a casual call for someone to go out and get sandwiches. At that point you are going to have to try and get something that's going to suit your palate and your planned calorie intake. If it's a regular event from your own office, then you know pretty much what the local options are, because you will have investigated them. Most firms tend to use the same sandwich bar for take-aways, so you need to check out their menu, so you can choose the options you need. This is just like doing the market research on your suppliers in business and deciding what you want from them.

If the meeting is outside your office, you must be specific about your needs because you have no idea what the local offerings may be. In that case, a safe bet is to go for something light like a smoked salmon sandwich without cream cheese, or salad with lean ham. You can also be flexible. For example, if you have gone for a cheese sandwich and the portion is generous, you don't have to eat all the cheese. Remember that you need the carbohydrate and fibre in bread, but go easy on the fat, so ask for low-fat spread and no mayonnaise. A boxed salad, baked potato (without butter) or sushi box would also be acceptable alternatives, if available.

If you are faced with a mixed buffet lunch being brought in, ask for a selection of fresh fruit as well. But if the buffet includes quiches, sausage rolls, pies and crisps, avoid or seriously limit these, as they are all high in fat. Drink plenty of water as that will also help to fill you up.

Quick checklist of suitable lunchtime options:

- Always think low-fat, low-calorie, and ask for low-fat spreads

- Plan ahead so you have a choice

- Try to get fruit included in the choice

- Avoid buffet foods that are high in fat, like quiche, sausages, roasted nuts and crisps

- Limit or avoid alcohol, and drink plenty of water

- Go for protein and salad combinations

- Avoid mayonnaise combinations like coronation chicken or prawn cocktail

---

Pubs and Wine Bars

Working lunches that are more social in nature often take place in pubs or wine bars. The emphasis is usually on something quick – with high-fat choices like sausages and chips, and beer to drink. In these more health-conscious days there will also be a salad alternative or a baked potato. The potato is a good option, because you can choose the type of topping you have with it and make it fit your eating plan. An ideal dietary combination is baked potato with baked beans or cottage cheese, but leave off the butter and other types of cheese.

Going out for drinks after work can cause difficulties, especially if everybody else is ordering pints of beer. If that's what you've always ordered in the past, then there is some culture change needed around that and that's one of the things you need to cope with. You need to be aware that that could be a painful situation. One way to cope with it is to be absolutely firm and up-front and just say 'I'm not drinking this evening'. This was how I did it and I found that so long as I was very clear and very strong about it, people didn't question it, just assuming I had a health issue I was working with. Or you can say you're not drinking alcohol because you are in training and have to get up early in the morning. Again, because people these days are both more health-conscious, and aware of the drink-driving laws, they tend not to give you hassle.

As always, the key to handling this is your attitude. Be absolutely decided and focused inside yourself, and you will not have a problem outside. Your body language and tone will reflect what is going on inside. Draw on all the resources you have created for yourself when you developed your Picture in Words (from Chapter 6), your Business Plan and the executive summary (from Chapter 5). Now is the time to start to draw on those inner strengths – this is payback time, when you reap the benefits of your hard work early on. This is the cutting edge of the battle. Succeed in these battles and ultimately you will win the war!

Restaurants and Hotels

Here you have the widest choice, whether you are having a business dinner, or a social evening with your partner or friends. With restaurants, try always to have a game plan, and think ahead. Divide restaurants broadly into two categories: fish or meat. Then you know you can ask for something plainly grilled, with not much oil or butter on it, even if it isn't on the menu. Ask for steamed vegetables, and plain potatoes or rice with it.

If you're eating Italian, you can have a starter of pasta with a light tomato sauce, followed by grilled meat or fish with a salad. In a French restaurant, talk to the waiter and describe what you want. Be enthusiastic; 'This is what I would *really* like' and describe the sort of meal you desire. Offer them a little bit of a challenge and, if it's a good restaurant, they will invariably oblige.

If you have no choice about where you are going to be eating, at a conference or after a meeting, it becomes much more difficult, when the group you're with vote for possibly high-calorie choices like Mexican or Indian. You have to calculate what you can choose off the menu – always looking for the low-fat, low-calorie option.

Here are some useful tips when you are faced with an unfamiliar restaurant:

- Avoid the bread basket. If you do take bread, have it in the French fashion without butter.

- Remember P for Plain, in other words, meat or fish without sauce.

- Load up on carbohydrates, such as plain boiled or baked potatoes, or pasta with a vegetable, not a creamy, sauce.

- Order first if you can, because that often sets the standard for what others will order and yours won't stand out. In mixed company that's not so easy because convention says that women go first, but in an all-male group, try to get your order in early.

- If you are in an Indian restaurant, order a meat tandoori with no sauce, and with plain rice it is relatively healthy. In a Chinese restaurant, go for boiled rice and steamed fish or vegetables. If people want to eat Oriental, try to go to Thai or Japanese restaurants, as the choices are nearer your dietary needs.

- If there really is nothing suitable for you, order the best option you can, and then eat only half of it. This will probably go unnoticed, or you can claim not to feel very hungry.

- Be confident and lighthearted about eating, and others will respond in the same way. If you don't make a big issue of it, then it's likely no one else will notice.

Alcohol

It's best to cut out alcohol altogether, from a nutritional point of view. However, on social occasions this can be awkward, so accept a small glass of wine and then pretend to sip it or have lots of water with it. This way you look as sociable as everyone else. The other option is to offer the excuse that you are driving. This will make you very popular at parties because you're always willing to drive and let others do the drinking!

If you think about alcohol as 'empty' calories, meaning it has less nutritional value, and can use up quite a bit of your daily allowance, it becomes easier to cut it out. I know that there are strong arguments about the benefits of red wine. This is if you have one glass, daily! How many of us regularly stick to that? The second point is that it can dull your perception. So you become less vigilant about checking your food and focusing on your weight management programme. You are also more likely to overeat if you are drinking.

Perhaps the best way to approach this is to adopt a no drinking policy at your new company – your body/business.

On Business Abroad

It can be difficult when you're travelling on business to countries where you don't know what's on offer. The best solution is to think strategically well ahead. Perhaps it's best to avoid restaurants completely if you can and buy yourself the basics of a healthy sandwich in a local supermarket.

Travel

By car

If you are out on the road driving, the same comments apply as to normal eating out. Either bring your own picnic or buy yourself a low-calorie, low-fat sandwich *en route*. When you stop to buy fuel, avoid picking up something 'to keep you going' on the way, whenever you can. Definitely make this the exception to the rule!

Think about the difference between the UK and the US on one hand, and France on the other. Petrol stations in France often sell no food at all, because there is no demand, as French people take their food seriously and proper meals are given high priority. Whereas in the UK and the US, most petrol stations sell a large variety of sugary, fatty snacks – and they have become a very lucrative sideline. What does that tell you about the world's obesity stakes?

By rail

When you travel by rail you are surrounded by temptation, and are perhaps slightly bored or stressed after a tiring day of meetings – all you want to do is relax a little and unwind. Try to remind yourself of your objectives and focus on the menu plan you have for that day. If you have planned to eat a meal in the buffet or restaurant car, there will usually be some healthy options to choose from: it's the snacking opportunities you have to watch out for.

By air

These days airlines are particularly good at providing a choice of meals. When booking your flight ask your PA or travel agent to order a 'special meal', one which is low-calorie and low-fat.

Avoid alcohol when flying, if you can. It only serves to dehydrate you further and will make it more difficult to recover from the flight at the other end. If you absolutely must have a drink, because you need to steady your nerves when flying, have plenty of water with it. The effects of the alcohol will be felt more quickly and you will become less dehydrated.

Keeping fit on the move

So much for the nutritional aspects of travel – but don't forget to exercise. Where you can, always book a hotel that will give you the facilities you require for your programme. If this is difficult, take some kit that will enable you to do at least some aerobic exercise and some muscle toning, for example, your training kit, heart monitor and a Dynaband. While these items take up very little room they are more than adequate for a good workout.

Or ask the hotel staff to advise you where there is a good run or walk locally. They will also be able to tell you about any no-go areas you should avoid. With that information at hand you can go off and explore – seeing far more than most business-men do on an average business trip.

Social events

When you're invited to a friend's house for dinner, you need to take the initiative straightaway. When you accept the invita-tion, say that you would love to come, and you hate to ask the question, but you are looking for something you can eat that will be low-calorie and low-fat. You may feel embarrassed or inhibited about that, but vegetarians, those with allergies and those who only eat kosher, have to mention their requirements too. And these days, paying attention to nutrition is so common that it's not considered a problem. Usually the host looks on it as a challenge to produce a special meal for everybody around your requirements.

If the occasion is less formal, such as a barbecue or a picnic, you can take your own low-fat food along. If friends suggest a take-away, state your preferences, having already done your homework (by reading this book!) on what foods you can eat.

Take-away options

- Nothing should be banned, because we all live in a real world, but it's sensible to try to avoid those fast-food, high-fat outlets, such as burger bars and fried chicken joints.

- Indian restaurants can pose problems as many of their dishes are cooked in lots of butter, cream or ghee, but you can choose steamed rice, and lighter options like chicken tandoori, which is baked in the oven.

- Chinese food has both good and bad options. Soups are often very nutritious and low-calorie, low-fat, and again you can choose steamed or boiled rice. Avoid deep-fried dishes and those with heavy sauces such as sweet and sour.

- Japanese food is a healthy option, although it is not available everywhere and can be very expensive.

- Thai food is a great take-away option, with many healthy, low-fat choices, and it is becoming more and more popular.

Special Occasions

Whatever the event, in your business or social life, the strategy is the same. The good thing here is that you always get plenty of notice, so whether it's a dinner at the Guildhall or a private celebration of a wedding or an anniversary, you have time to plan ahead. These events usually have a fixed menu, so find out who the caterers are, and ask them for a low-calorie, low-fat version of the meal. Caterers are very familiar with such requests from people with allergies and special dietary requirements like vegetarian or kosher. If the menu is totally fixed, you can still ask to have the meat or fish without the cream sauce.

Holidays

The Warriors weight management programme is all about you not being on or off a diet, but just eating normally for the rest of your life. So when you go on holiday, do enjoy yourself, but always keep your eye on your overall objectives in relation to food. It's not so much a case of 'a little of what you fancy does you good', but the concept of looking closely at what you are trying to achieve.

When faced with rich food on holiday, filter it through the concept of 'Is this the supply that I want to let into my factory, and is this the raw material I really need, to manufacture the widgets that I genuinely want to produce?'. Looked at from that point of view, and however delicious and palatable, if you ask yourself, 'Is this right for me?', you'll quickly find the answer. If it's a little bit of chocolate here or a particularly rich, creamy sauce with pasta there, that's not a problem, your body/ business can deal with that on an occasional basis. It doesn't matter, and it's no big deal! Just keep in mind that you are trying to maintain your weight comfortably, so you can have these treats more frequently because you're not trying to lose weight. Even if you are cutting back on the calories, nothing is prohibited and you deserve to enjoy your holidays to the utmost – just try not to make them a culinary extravaganza!

Other Potential Problems

The main problem area, sadly, is often other people. They will try to convince you that you could give yourself a treat, allow yourself off the hook, and have that special thing that everyone else is having. There's a bit of a power game going on here, to see whether you can be shown to be weak. So the best way to overcome it is to be very clear, very focused and very determined, and nobody stands in your way. It's when you vacillate that they see the chink in your armour and they go for it.

Think of the Japanese Samurai warriors. They rarely had to fight. Their inner strength and resolve were so powerful that their mere presence was sufficient to instill enormous respect in the onlooker.

Key points

- Be confident and clear about your food choices, and others will not question you about them.

- Plan, plan and plan again to make sure you get what you require from business, social or celebratory occasions.

- On road trips, pack a healthy picnic lunch to take with you.

- Take minimal, essential exercise equipment with you on trips.

- Be firm and positive (and keep off the alcohol) and you won't succumb to temptation.

11
Mind-set II

Objectives

- To learn how to get back on track

- To identify (or re-identify) what really drives you

- To learn how to cope with temporary failure, and not to punish yourself

- To learn how to control binge attacks

This chapter is about how to cope when you hit crisis point. This is something that happens to everyone at some point in the Warriors programme. What are you going to do when you have lost the motivation and focus you started out with? Here's how to get right back on track.

What's Driving You?

In your business you have to know what motivates you and what makes things happen – whether it's meeting targets or overcoming the competition. It's the same with your body/business – you have to know the reasons why you want to lose weight. The deeper and stronger those reasons are, and the clearer your focus, the more likely you are to succeed. Most men who undertake a weight management programme are driven by one of two forces: fear or pleasure.

Motivated by fear?

Fear is usually the strongest motivator for men who want to lose weight. They are aware that they have – or could have – potentially life-threatening medical conditions arising out of being overweight. They may have had a medical scare and been warned by their doctors that, unless they change their behaviour and lose their excess weight, they won't be around in a few years' time.

Motivated by pleasure?

An equally valid motivator is pleasure, and this can be a great driving force too. Perhaps the idea of visualising yourself as a fit athlete is one of your strongest driving forces, or perhaps you have a mental idea of stripping off on the beach and not having to hide under a towel.

What's your internal motivation?

These fear or pleasure factors need to be mapped out by you, as an individual. They cannot be prescribed; they are things that are inside you. It is this internal motivation that is so important. You can, and probably have been, driven by external motivators and they do work, but only for a while. External driving forces can be infinitely varied, from advertising around body image to a nagging partner or family, and they can end up having a negative effect. The real key is to decide, inside yourself, what you feel is right and when you've decided that, you will be in the right frame of mind to draw upon your real strengths.

Whether your internal driving force is fear or pleasure, or sometimes even a combination of both, you have to understand what is motivating you. External forces leave you too vulnerable to change and are far too fickle to be reliable. Somebody or something else is doing the driving, when you really want to be in the driving seat yourself, with your hands firmly on the steering wheel.

Look at Your Motivation

What was really motivating you when you bought this book and decided to start on the Warriors programme? Have a look in your notebook at the Picture in Words you worked on in Chapter 6, together with your Business Plan from Chapter 5.

Take a fresh page and head it: 'Mind-set – what's driving me'. Now write down all your reasons for wanting to lose weight and get fit – large and small, significant and frivolous – under the headings of fear and pleasure. Also, note if they are externally or internally driven. Ask yourself the following questions:

- What benefits would you get from a healthier body (pleasure)?

- What are the problems and drawbacks of being overweight (fear)?

- What are all the reasons why you absolutely must lose weight? Make these as strong as you can, because the stronger the vision around both the fear and the pleasure, the more you will be ready for change and the more likely you will be to succeed.

Below, you will find my own thoughts about my initial weight-loss motivators:

Fear	Internal/External	Pleasure	Internal/External
Heart attack	Internal	Sport	Internal
Getting teased	External	Comment on looks	External
Low self-esteem	Internal	Great energy	Internal
Medical health warning	External		
Going for a new job	External		
Afraid my body can't do it	Internal	But I really want to run a marathon	

Now, use your imagination to think what life will be like when you have a healthy body, the one you really want. Imagine what it will feel like when you are in that body and what you will be able to do. That will help to clarify why you are doing this programme. Now write it down in your notebook.

What are the Benefits of Being Overweight?

No, I haven't gone mad! If you think about it, there must be some benefits, otherwise you would not be overweight! Perhaps you feel insecure and have low self-esteem. By being over-weight, do you come across as being extremely powerful, without having to use your personality to do it? Think about what the benefits are for you and ask yourself these questions:

- Are these 'real' benefits?

- Do they enable you to achieve your objectives, as set out in your Business Plan?

- Do they conflict with the vision that you have of the future, as set out in your Picture in Words?

If you find that there is a substantial conflict between these perceived benefits and what your identified objectives are, then it may be the right time to discuss that conflict with a profes-sional, for example, a counsellor or a lifestyle coach (visit the Warriors website, see Useful Addresses, page 186).

> Whatever your reasons for being overweight, it is impor-tant to realise what they are, because these are things that will tend to trip you up later on when you're having some success with your programme.

Still in a Fix?

All right – you know what's driving you, and you know all the theory, but it's still going wrong! Hope is not lost. This is how to cope in a crisis.

When crisis hits, and it always does, there are certain key things that you can do to get yourself out of the situation, and back on track. Your internal dialogue is one of the crucial factors here.

There are essentially two levels on which to act:

1. How to break the pattern when it hits.
2. How to manage your life so that the situation arises with less frequency and less intensity in the future.

This is comparable in business to the power going down. As a manager, your first concern would be to get it back on, and get the company working again. Then, once things are back to 'normal', you would sit back and analyse what had gone wrong and what you could do to ensure that the power did not fail again. Your analysis might show that this was a situation that was caused by something outside your control. It may have been the generator that supplied your company that had a problem. You may need, therefore, to change your generator or to agree a plan of action to ensure that you receive the supply of power you require. Or, you may find that the fault lies within your own company. There may be problems with the wiring and that is why the lights went off.

Now relate this to your body/business. This is how the various stages compare:

1. You came home from work and got stuck into a binge – the lights in the factory went out!

2. You then decided you have to get the lights back on *immediately*. You stopped half-way through the binge (this is very powerful as it builds confidence and a strong mental muscle) – the lights came back on.

3. You analyse the possible reasons for having the binge:
   • The first reason was that you had had a rotten day at work and

one of your suppliers had let you down (stress) – the generator failed to supply electricity.

- The second reason was that you were tired and you had nothing else to do at that time of night (boredom) – the company's wiring was faulty.

When Things Go Off Track

When things go wrong on the Warriors weight management programme it is because you have not managed to live up to its commitments and the standards you first set for yourself. Remember the three key areas, when looking at whether you will succeed:

- **Nutrition**   Are you eating outside the parameters of what you had planned to eat and need to eat? Is this failure due to the quantity (portion size); the quality (too high in fat); or the location (outside the time you had planned to eat)?

- **Exercise**   Did you plan to do it, but for some reason were unable to?

- **Planning and review**   Did you not manage to make the time available to plan and review the programme? This might be due to the fact that you were unable to keep the food and mood diary up-to-date. Or, you may not have had time to plan your meals for the following week. Perhaps boredom set in and you just couldn't be bothered to do the planning and the review.

Everyone slips up from time to time. The important thing is not that you slip up – it's how you decide to cope when you do so.

Don't beat yourself up!

Men have a tendency to beat themselves up when they have failed to follow through on a plan. Ask yourself, how much good does beating yourself up do? Consider a similar situation in a business environment. Think of how you would treat a new member of your staff in similar circumstances. Consider, for a moment, how you would treat him, if he got things wrong in his first few months. If you came down on him like a ton of bricks, which is what you may well do (internally) with yourself when you slip up, what type of a culture would you have created within your company? What would morale be like? How would your staff respond in the future? Either they would quit – which is what most people do when things go wrong in weight management – they give up! Or, you would soldier on, miserable and depressed, until there comes a point when you can no longer cope, and you're fired.

What would you prefer – to give up or get fired? I am sure you would rather be given as many chances as you need, until you get it right. Put yourself in the shoes of a good boss, and ask yourself how you would treat your new manager. Answer these questions:

- Would you be compassionate?
- Would you be understanding?
- Would you encourage the manager to do better?
- Would you want to be firm but forgiving?
- Would you try to maintain morale, but at the same time maintain discipline, to ensure that the results of the business are achieved?

So, just like any other human being, you have gone off track. This is what you have to do:

- Recognise that things have gone wrong

- Make a serious effort to get back on track as quickly as possible. Do not give up!

- Understand what went wrong and how to avoid a recurrence of the same situation in the future.

- Finally, ask yourself – 'What can I learn from this experience?'

Reasons Why You Go Off Track

By now you will know that the three factors that can cause you to go off track on a weight management programme are stress, habit and boredom. When things go wrong, ask yourself which one of the three is coming into play.

In our earlier example of the early evening binge, which we compared with a factory power cut, two factors came into play – stress and boredom. Here are some of the more common habit-related factors:

- **Nibbling**   You might do this in front of the TV, diving into the nut dish at the bar, or always having a biscuit with your coffee.

- **Driving**   Buying a snack to eat when you pay for your petrol.

- **Drinking**   after work.

- **Bread rolls**   in a restaurant.

Your Food and Mood Diary

This tool, which we looked at in Chapter 3, is vital when dealing with a weight management crisis. The difference between keeping this little book up-to-date and being a successful weight manager, and letting it slide, forgotten in the back drawer of a desk, is like the difference between night and day. Why?

- Because it helps to focus the mind on what you are doing with food when you keep that part of the programme up-to-date.

- Because it enables you to see the patterns around your eating when you go off track.

If you have stopped using your food and mood diary, and you find that things are beginning to slip, do not hesitate to fish it out again and use it. Anyone who has successfully managed their weight invariably has some way of keeping a constant running record of what they are doing with food, monitoring what they eat, when they eat and how much. Many of the most successful weight managers also analyse the reasons why they go off track and learn from their experience. It's often said, 'It's not what you're eating, it's what is eating you' – when you write down your food and your mood, it will tell you that.

How to Cope When You Hit a Binge

- Do you ever get the feeling that you have to eat a particular thing and that you have to have it, right now?

- Do you ever feel that somehow the food in the fridge is calling you, saying – 'Eat me!'

- Do you ever feel that the urge to eat a bar of chocolate is so strong that you have ceased to have control of the situation?

You need to recognise these signs as precursors to a binge. Think of some instances when you have had an urge to binge.

- What goes through your mind?
- What are the things that set you off? Is it a particular situation or food?
- Is there a time when this happens more frequently?

These are all valuable notes to make in your food and mood diary, as they happen – day-to-day. Still, knowing all this, the urges keep coming – what can you do? Try these two suggestions. The first is called 'distance, distract, time' and the second uses your mood to focus on your body.

Distance, distract, time

First, try to move, physically, as far away as possible from whatever it is that is causing the problem. For example, move away from the fridge, if you are at home, and keep away from the bar and the canapés if you are out at a party. Keep your **distance**.

Then, do anything you can to take your mind off the situation. Listen to music. Have a bath. Go for a walk. Do some exercise. Read a book. Try some breathing exercises. Meditate. Light a scented candle (smell can quickly change mood). Surf the Internet. Play patience. Get physical – punch a pillow or, better still, your punch bag. If you have a hobby that gives you great pleasure – do it. If not, take up a hobby that you would enjoy at these times. Do whatever it takes to **distract** your mind so that your focus goes elsewhere. If you can change your focus for even a short period, say 20 to 30 minutes, it's surprising how the urge to binge passes.

Finally, set a **time** by when you will allow yourself to binge. I know this sounds crazy, but try it! Say to yourself – 'I shall have that (whatever it is you want) in (however long – say (at least) 30 minutes.)'. After that time try asking yourself these questions:

- Now that I can have it, do I really want it?

- What will this do to the other plans I have for my body, and what I want out of it?

Think about your commitment to yourself. Have a look at your Picture in Words, if you have it to hand. The chances are you will have overcome the urge and while it 'would be nice' to have whatever it was, it is no longer a compulsion! You are once more back in control and can cope.

Use your mood to focus on your body

Allow yourself to focus in and see what information your body is giving you. Use the mood that you are feeling, when you feel the urge to binge, or go off track, to listen into your body and see what it is trying to tell you. Moods are generally designed to be messengers. They function as a wake-up call for action. It is your body's way of telling you to do something. Find out what it is trying to tell you and work with it.

The worst-case scenario

Let's now look at the worst-case scenario – when you succumb to a binge! In spite of all your good intentions, it happens – you cannot resist and you start bingeing. You can choose to stop yourself from doing that! This is one of the most powerful things that you can do. When you are right in the middle of a binge and you have the strength of mind and will to break off, you will not only have regained control, you will have started to build a very valuable mental muscle. You will notice that, once you have the ability to do that, and do it more and more often, your sense of control over the situation will grow. Fairly soon you will start to feel you no longer have the 'compulsion' to binge – it has become a choice.

To start this process, always ask yourself questions, while you are bingeing, like:

- Is this my only option – right now?
- Do I really want (whatever it is I am eating)?
- What is this food or drink doing to me?
- Is this going to get me any closer to what I want my body to do for me?

If it helps, copy these questions and stick them wherever you are likely to see them when you experience a binge – perhaps the fridge or larder door. Remember that the idea is to stop yourself in the middle of the act, not find yourself saying 'Oh, what the hell – just this once! I'll shape up tomorrow'.

Dangerous Situations

There are plenty of obvious things that can send us off track. Just being around 'trigger foods', the ones that we find irresistible, can do it. There are, however, other situations, some much subtler, which you should consider, and these are listed below.

Transitions

Whenever we move from one environment to another somehow our guard is lowered and there will be a tendency to 'feel the urge to eat'. This could be moving from office to home. Going into the executive lounge at an airport before a flight. Arriving at a hotel and settling down into the new room. Leaving work with some colleagues and, on the spur of the moment, deciding to go for a drink or a quick meal. What are your 'transitions'? Think of the times when you move from one environment to another and what that does to your appetite. Are there areas where you need to be on your guard because they trigger moments of weakness?

Friends and family

Is there someone in the family who insists, in the 'nicest possible way', that you have whatever has been made specially for you? Do you ever hear any of these comments?

- A little of what you fancy does you good.
- Once in a while won't matter.
- Ease up on yourself. It's the weekend, relax, don't be so hard on yourself.
- You're overdoing things on that diet of yours.
- You're losing weight far too fast – you'll damage your health.

This list could go on and on, but the important thing to recognise is that all of these things will blow you off course. Here are some suggestions to help you cope in these situations.

- Look back to Chapter 10 for advice on dealing with the potential problems of eating out, whether at work or with friends and family.

- Get focused and be firm. Invariably, I have found that, if I am inwardly strong others sense it and 'don't mess with me'. This comes from believing in and being clear about your Business Plan and your Picture in Words, and reflecting that in what you say.

- If people sometimes try to 'play games' with you, by saying 'You're on a diet – you're not allowed that', remember, you are allowed everything, but you choose not to have it now. It's like inappropriate stock turning up at your factory gate; you just don't need it, nor do you want it, even if the factory could take it in! It's also important to get the other person off your back. When you tell them that you can have everything, that soon shuts them up!

- Do you ever comfort eat because you are in pain? Recognise that you are in pain and deal with it in the most appropriate way that does not involve food.

- Do you sometimes eat sugary foods to give yourself an energy boost? If so, you need to get some rest! Your body is telling you it needs it. If you are feeling tired and still have to carry on, try some deep breathing exercises. The way to do this is on a ratio of 1:4:2. That is breathing in for a count of 1, holding for 4, and breathing out for 2. What is important is that the ratio stays the same, however long the first breath lasts. The easiest way to do that is by counting the numbers of seconds, just as long as you are consistent with the ratio of 1:4:2. Repeat the process three times to restore your energy levels. Or get your circulation moving by doing some very brisk exercise for a minute or two. These exercises will not keep you awake all night, but they will give you as much of a temporary energy boost as any bar of chocolate!

Key points

- Everyone falls off the Warriors programme at some point or other, so don't beat yourself up for it.

- Get absolutely clear on your fear/pleasure motivators; they will keep you on track.

- Identify whether it's stress, habit or boredom that causes you to get distracted from the programme or brings on a binge.

- You always have a choice about what you eat, and how much of it. You are in the driving seat.

- Stay focused and firm about your objectives.

12
Never Stop Managing

Objectives

- To know how to maintain the success you have achieved

- To be able to beat the temptation to let things slip

- To recognise the importance of what you have achieved

Now you understand the theory of the Warriors programme – it's time to begin the practice.

Although this is the final chapter in the book, it really is only the beginning. Losing weight and getting fit are only the first stage of any weight management programme. It's staying that way that can often present the greatest challenge. I know this only too well, because all my life food has been my coping mechanism. Whenever I'm under pressure, food is where I've found refuge. Like most business executives, I am under considerable pressure much of the time. At the time of writing this book, I had four full-time projects under way, including the running of two businesses. Old habits die hard, comfort eating began to set in and I noticed my weight beginning to creep up. So this chapter is absolutely based on my experience of dealing with pressure and learning how to keep myself on track.

The Vicious Cycle

Those terrible 'shoulds' and 'musts' are ever present when we think about weight management – and yet they benefit us very little in practice. First, you have to find ways of lowering the emotional temperature that is around your weight. Your initial instinct is to beat yourself up, especially when you find your clothes are getting tight. You tell yourself you're a failure and weak-willed. And you worry that other people are noticing the increase too. With all that pressure on you, as you start on the slippery slide back, your instinct is to revert to the one comfort that you've always recognised – food. You know that if you 'treat' yourself to a nice high-fat, unhealthy meal it will cheer you up, but of course it also sets off the vicious cycle of out-of-control eating again and builds all the more negative pressure. You need to try to defuse that pressure.

A much calmer, rational and observing standpoint would be to say, 'Yes, I do care, I really want to do something about this and get back on track, because if I don't I'm not going to achieve the goals and objectives that I've set'. If you put yourself into panic mode and get into that cycle, where you beat yourself up, that's where things start to go badly wrong. Blame, guilt and anger at yourself simply don't help in this situation. It's not that you don't care – in fact you care deeply – but it is important to be aware of the way in which you care, and how you talk to yourself. Ask yourself:

- Is my voice that of a kind, supportive coach?

- Or am I giving free rein to that really vicious critical judge who sits inside most of us, saying things like 'I should lose weight', 'I must exercise more', 'I should not have eaten that' and 'I must not snack between meals'?

Those harsh inner voices are often the worst enemy of all. They only serve to undermine us and our best endeavours.

Accentuate the Positive

So, instead of beating yourself up, what else can you do? Concentrate on enjoying a sense of achievement. Remember that you have reached your original goals of losing weight and getting fitter, healthier and happier.

Your friends and family will heap praise on you while you are undergoing the process of adopting new habits, especially when they can see the weight dropping off you. Then of course it becomes the norm, so they stop commenting. There would appear to be no prizes for weight maintenance, so if you thrive on recognition you can begin to feel rather empty, and return to comfort eating again – the old coping mechanism!

It's important to look for praise and recognition internally, not externally. It's about being able to sense deeply what the goals and objectives are for yourself, not for somebody else. That is why all the work you did, in the Business Plan and the Picture in Words, is so valuable. When you achieve your objectives you really recognise, inside, that it's all been worthwhile. If it doesn't come from inside you, then you're open to long-term failure because external sources of encouragement and praise all too soon evaporate.

The way to break this cycle is by making sure you give *yourself* great recognition for achieving your goals. Enjoy the praise that might be coming from outside while it lasts; accept it but don't build too much on it and don't overplay it. Allow yourself to feel terrific, but only because it's reinforcing what you want inside.

Listen to Your Inner Coach

Do not allow that critical inner judge to rule. Temper it into the strong but compassionate voice of a superb coach – one who always encourages you to win. Find your inner voice. One that recognises where you came off track and, without letting you off the hook, reminds you how to get back on track. Stand outside yourself and look at yourself as a person you really want to succeed, then think of what you would say to that person when things are not on track.

Remind yourself that for successful weight and fitness management, you must think of it as:

- a gradual process

- more like a war than a battle, which can only be won by always staying with it and never giving in, and

- it does not matter how many times you break your rules – so long as you *learn from the experience* and keep going forward.

Like any company director or CEO you get to know how Your Body Ltd runs, so the process will get easier, but you can never stop managing it. In all businesses, circumstances change and you need to respond. There may be peaks and troughs in your progress graph. In your body business the troughs could be represented by Christmas or other celebrations, when you may be eating foods outside your normal patterns or unable to follow your exercise routine. Recognise that these troughs are only temporary aberrations, plan ahead for them if you can, and adjust accordingly.

Coping Mechanisms

If your method of coping has always been through food, then you need to shift your behaviour and adopt better alternatives. What else can be a source of your nurturing, if it's not food? We have already looked at some possibilities in Chapter 11, but here are some reminders. If it can't be food, could it be:

talking to a friend	listening to music
exercise	going for a walk
playing cards	reading a book or magazine
having a relaxing bath	playing a board or computer game
going out to a concert	seeing a film

You might use some, or all, of these things at different times. If you are turning to food because you are angry, then some physical activity might help defuse it. If you are feeling sad, lonely or unappreciated, talking to a friend may be the answer. What you have to do is short-circuit the automatic response to problems. Start keeping a list of the other things that you can do that will break the cycle.

The treats jar

One of the methods I used was to have a treats jar. I made a list of all the things I enjoyed that would distract me from food. I wrote them down on separate slips of paper, folded them and put them into a jar. When I needed a boost, or had just gone through a hard time, I would put my hand in and pick out one thing at random. My treats included things like going to the cinema, a visit to a bookshop, or lying on the sofa listening to a favourite piece of music. Whatever was on my list had to provide some instant gratification.

The 3-D Technique

Apart from just dealing with the immediate problem of discomfort around food, or needing a bit of self-nurturing, by finding a distraction like playing cards or a computer game, you also need to ask yourself 'Why am I getting this message?' These messages are actually your friends. They are little wake-up calls, and they're trying to tell you something. So even if it's uncomfortable and you don't like the feelings you're getting, listen in to them and try to work with whatever the feeling or mood is telling you.

Try this shorthand reminder of the 3-D technique we looked at in Chapter 11:

- **Discomfort:** remind yourself of your goals – look again at your Mission Statement

- **Distance:** step physically away from the presence of food – move to another room, if possible

- **Distraction:** find alternative ways of getting your needs met other than through food.

Get Back to Basics

You can't afford to be complacent because you have reached your target weight or fitness goals. You need to be managing this business all the time, but of course it will vary in the input you have to give it. As with any business, the intensity of input gets easier because your understanding becomes greater. To keep yourself on track becomes a simpler process because of that understanding, but never forget that you can always go back to where you were if you stop managing the business that is your body.

If you think you are losing momentum and could go back to your old eating habits, just step outside yourself, take a look at what your body/business is about and get back to basics. If things start going out of kilter, look at what you were doing that was successful up to the point where you slid back and do whatever is needed to get yourself back on track. These three factors could be the keys to re-establishing your healthy routine:

1. **You must reduce portion sizes.** Don't change what you are eating, because you should be eating an essentially healthy balanced diet of the things that you really enjoy, just eat less. The Warriors programme is about long-term healthy living, so if you're going wrong in terms of your weight control then the real question is portion size more than anything else. If you're eating more than the standard three meals a day, or having lots of snacks, then that's another thing to look at.

2. **Increase the intensity and duration of exercise**. This is how you are going to burn up those extra calories. For best effect you should be doing at least three 30-minute sessions a week and taking every opportunity to get in some aerobic activity – including running for the bus!

3. **Take a close look at what has caused you to come off track**. This means going back through your exercise and food logs, paying particular attention to the mood aspects of your behaviour.

Drawing the Line

If your clothes are getting too tight, do not go out and buy a bigger size. *Resolve absolutely* to make those clothes comfortable again. Analyse the situation and think of all the things you could do. You could get out your Picture in Words and remind yourself of all the reasons why you started this process and how you do not want to be back at the beginning again.

Catch yourself early. Most people manage their weight, but the difference is that people with a weight problem tend to let it go much further and have to take far bigger and more drastic action later on. They do not tend to take early action, whereas people who tend to be successful at managing their weight take action much sooner, at the first sign of their clothes getting a little bit tight.

It's a question of where you put your boundaries. Where is your tolerance line? Because you are going to hit it at some stage, if you start to regress. When you find that you're going adrift, click into action very early on. At the first sign of a couple of pounds (say 1kg) over, that's your click-in mechanism, don't let it go beyond there. At that stage it is not going to be as much effort to correct, but let it slide and it is tough. I know, because I've been through it myself, but I also recognise that unless I catch the slide early on, it's going to be the long-term slog yet again, and there is no way I am going back to weighing over 22 stones.

The Rest of the Journey

Weight management is a journey, which for some will possibly be the most difficult journey they will ever have to make in their lives. It is a battle with yourself and how you deal with life. Once you can deal with these issues, conquer them and put them behind you, you will also find that you have taken control of your life as well.

Also remember that over a period of time you'll find your goals and objectives change. When you started, you might have thought your ultimate goal was to run a 10km (6.2 miles) race. Then you find you've done that, and now you want to do a 50km (31 miles) race. Goals change and you need to respond accordingly. You need to decide what sort of eating pattern you require and what sort of increased training you have to put in. It may be that what you set yourself originally just isn't in tune with what you really want. You may have gone through a learning process where you've discovered that although your original goals and objectives were very valid, with experience they've changed. That's perfectly acceptable, you just need to adjust your plan to fit the new parameters.

The Last Word

Undertaking this programme is not just a one-off. Looking back to how you were in the beginning, you will see that healthy eating, exercise and a positive attitude to your body has now become a way of life for you. You are no longer going to be on or off a diet; your eating habits are now a consistent and integrated part of your whole life. You are always going towards your goals, which are in harmony with your stated objective of having a healthier, fitter and happier life. If you are not doing that it tells you something about how you need to adjust any aspect of your programme to reflect that harmony.

Having understood the programme and set it in motion, if there is a problem all you need to do is some fine-tuning, not have a radical change or relaunch. Once you've understood this approach to weight management you realise that it is not about yo-yo dieting or impossible eating programmes, where you are lurching from one major diet method to another huge diet effort. From now on what you're doing is fine-tuning all the time and getting yourself back on to your path. There is no great radical change because the strategy you have built is now a consistent approach and is totally integrated with your lifestyle.

So there you go – it's simple! Concentrate on putting what you have learned into practice, and the rest will follow.

My top ten keys to long-term success

1. **Don't dwell on what went wrong.** Learn from it and put it behind you. If, at any stage, you find you are slipping and the programme is not working, go back to the things that did work – sharpen up your focus again and look at the basics; exercise, nutrition and monitoring.

2. **Spend plenty of time on your successes.** Make something out of them. Find ways to reward yourself for doing it right and getting to your short-term goals. Try to set the goals so that they are at least achievable – there is great power in feeling that you have actually over-achieved.

3. **Don't beat yourself up for not doing things right.** Give yourself every bit of encouragement to keep going and only use the past as a way of learning how to do it better.

4. **Plan your food consumption.** Be aware of how much you need; when to consume and where. Note

any changes to the plan so that you can see if there is a pattern or habit that needs to be changed or even broken.

5. **Take regular exercise that you enjoy.** Don't go for activities that give you no pleasure just because they're meant to do you good. If you have always hated the very thought of exercise then at least look for ways to make it less painful by adding in a social dimension. For example, go walking with friends, or go dancing with a partner whose company you relish. Or take a Walkman to the gym and listen to your favourite music, or listen to tapes of books you may not always have time to read.

6. **Keep your focus.** Always remind yourself what you want to do with your body and why. Never forget you have a choice and that choice is yours and yours alone. Think about getting the balance right between where you want to get to and the price you are willing to pay to get there. Accept the choice you make. Do not give yourself mixed messages – for example, wanting the 'perfect body' and at the same time not having enough hours in the day to work out, to the point where that is achievable, because the job and the family have to fit in somewhere too!

7. **Remember that life is not perfect, and nor are people.** Sometimes compromises are necessary.

8. **Get the important things into your life first.** The rest will always find a way to fill in the gaps. If you don't get those key things in, they will often not get into your life at all.

9. Remember you are not alone. You can build a team around you who will help you with your goals. You can join one of the many Warriors courses that will enable you to see the programme in action and meet others who could form a valuable support group for you.

10. Have an 'inner coach' to guide and support you. This figure can be with you, if you will let him, at all times.

Most of all, have fun and enjoy your Warriors programme. It has a very serious purpose, of course – it saved my life, and you may well find that it saves yours too!

Useful Addresses

Warriors

Visit the website:

www.warriors.org.uk

for full information on:

- How to order your Warriors Kit
- Where to find suitable coaches; personal trainers and nutritionists
- How to have your diet analysed by a professional nutritionist and advice about what to eat for optimum health
- Where you can find suitable equipment for training
- How to book on to one of the Warriors courses

If you are not on the Internet or do not have access to it then you can always contact Warriors as follows:

By telephone: 020 7266 2010

By fax: 020 7266 0366

By post: 264A Elgin Avenue, Maida Vale, London W9 1JR

Other Useful Addresses

UK

Alcohol Concern

Waterbridge House, 32–36 Loman Street, London SE1 0EE.
Tel: 020 7928 7377.
Drinkline: 0800 917 8282
Website: www.alcoholconcern.org.uk
This is a national voluntary agency working against alcohol
misuse. Members receive a regular magazine and have access
to extensive information and training services.

Alcoholics Anonymous (AA)

England and Wales: PO Box 1, Stonebow House, Stonebow,
York YO1 7NJ. Tel: 01904 644026. Fax: 01904 629091
Scotland: Baltic Chambers, 50 Wellington Street, Glasgow
G2 6HJ. Tel: 0141 226 2214
Website: www.alcoholics-anonymous.org.uk
AA started in Great Britain in 1947 and now has more than
2,000,000 members in 115 countries. If you have an alcohol
problem and want to stop drinking, you can become a member
and follow the Twelve Steps of recovery. Contact the General
Service Offices above to find out details of your local branch.

ASH (Action on Smoking and Health)

102 Clifton Street, London EC2A 4HW. Tel: 020 7739 5902.
Fax: 020 7613 0331
E-mail: action.smoking.health@dial.pipex.com
Website: www.ash.org.uk
ASH is a national organisation, with branches throughout the
United Kingdom. It is part of the global ASH movement
campaigning for policies to combat the dangers of tobacco
and smoking. They also have a range of publications and
videos for sale.

British Dietetic Association (BDA)

5th Floor, Charles House, 148–9 Great Charles Street, Birmingham B3 3HT. Tel: 0121 200 8080. Fax: 0121 200 8081.
E-mail: info@bda.uk.com
Website: www.bda.uk.com
There are approximately 5,000 State Registered Dietitians in the UK at present and the qualification is widely regarded as the gold standard in the industry. At Warriors most of our nutritionists are State Registered.

British Heart Foundation (BHF)

14 Fitzhardinge Street, London W1H 6DH. Tel: 020 7935 0185. Fax: 020 7486 5820.
Website: www.bhf.org.uk
Founded in 1961, The British Heart Foundation is the UK's leading heart charity. It aims to play a leading role in the fight against heart disease through research, education and providing support and information to heart patients and their families.

British Nutrition Foundation

High Holborn House, 52–54 High Holborn, London WC1V 6RQ. Tel: 020 7404 6504. Fax: 020 7404 6747.
E-mail: postbox@nutrition.org.uk
Website: www.nutrition.org.uk
They produce an information leaflet on coronary heart disease; a list of other publications is available on request.

BUPA

BUPA House, 15–19 Bloomsbury Way, London WC1A 2BA.
Tel: 020 7656 2000.
Websites: www.bupa.co.uk (for BUPA UK) or www.bupa.com (for BUPA worldwide).
Offers a range of private healthcare plans and advice to members. Can also arrange for health checks and medicals.

Consumers' Association (Which?)

2 Marylebone Road, London NW1 4DF. Tel: 020 7486 5544.
Fax: 020 7770 7600. Customer Service (9am–9pm Monday to
Friday, 9am–3pm Saturday): 0645 830 240
E-mail: which@which.net
Website: www.which.net

Coronary Prevention Group (CPG)

2 Taviton Street, London WC1H 0BT. Tel: 020 7927 2125.
Fax: 020 7927 2127.
E-mail: cpg@lshtm.ac.uk
Websites: www.healthnet.org.uk or www.healthpro.org.uk
The CPG was the first British charity devoted to the
prevention of coronary heart disease. They produce booklets
on coronary heart disease and are now developing more
educational material in electronic form.

Department of Health

Richmond House, 79 Whitehall, London SW1A 2NL. Public
Enquiry Office (10am–5pm Monday to Friday): 020 7210 4850
E-mail: dhmail@doh.gsi.gov.uk
Website: www.doh.gov.uk
This is the government department responsible for health.

Diabetes UK (formerly The British Diabetic Association)

Central Office, 10 Queen Anne Street, London W1G 9LH. Tel:
020 7323 1531. Fax: 020 7637 3644.
E-mail: info@diabetes.org.uk
BDA Careline (9am–5pm weekdays): 020 7636 6112 or
e-mail: careline@diabetes.org.uk
Website: www.diabetes.org.uk
Diabetes UK offers information and support on all aspects of
diabetes, but cannot comment on an individual person's
medical treatment. They have national and regional offices
throughout the UK.

Family Heart Association (FHA)

7 North Road, Maidenhead, Berkshire SL6 1PE. Tel: 01628
628 638. Fax: 01628 628 698.
E-mail: ad@familyheart.org
Website: www.familyheart.org
The FHA will help anyone at high risk of a heart attack, but
specialises in inherited conditions causing high cholesterol
(such as familial hypercholesterolaemia). Please note, for
general enquiries letters are preferred to phone calls.

Health Information Service

Tel: 0800 665544. This is the national helpline funded by
Health Authorities. Calls are diverted to local offices. Staff can
give information but are not medically trained.

Institute for Optimum Nutrition (ION)

Blades Court, Deodar Road, London SW15 2NU. Tel: 020 8877
9993. Fax: 020 8877 9980.
E-mail: info@ion.ac.uk
Website: www.ion.ac.uk
ION aims to educate both the general public and health
professionals about nutritional therapy.

MIND (National Association for Mental Health)

Granta House, 15–19 Broadway, Stratford, London E15 4BQ.
Tel: 020 8519 2122. Fax: 020 8522 1725.
E-mail: contact@mind.org.uk
Website: www.mind.org.uk
MIND is a mental health charity working for a better life for
everyone experiencing mental distress.

National Association of Citizens Advice Bureaux

Myddleton House, 115–123 Pentonville Road, London N1 9LZ.
Tel: 020 7833 2181. Fax: 020 7833 4371.
The Citizens Advice Bureaux Service offers free independent
and confidential advice on a whole range of problems

including consumer issues and legal matters. The address and telephone number of your local CAB will be in the phone book and in Yellow Pages under 'Counselling and Advice'.

Polar Heart Rate Monitors
For more information and for your local dealer listings please visit www.polar-uk.com or for mail order, tel: 01926 816155. Polar are the world leaders in Heart Rate Monitoring technology, providing a wide range of products to make exercise and training more safe and effective for everyone. The entry-level A-Series is ideal for general exercise, the M-Series is geared towards improving fitness levels and weight management, and the new S-Series (with cycling specific models) provides new technology to enhance training through precision testing, measuring and analysing.

PPP Healthcare
Phillips House, Crescent Road, Tunbridge Wells, Kent TN1 2PL. Tel: 0800 335555 for General Enquiries.
Website: www.ppphealthcare.co.uk (for PPP UK) or www.ppphealthcare.com (for PPP International)

Quit
Victory House, 170 Tottenham Court Road, London W1T 7NR Tel: 020 7388 5775. Freephone Quitline: 0800 002200.
E-mail: quit-projects@clara.co.uk
Website: www.quit.org.uk
Quit is a charity dedicated to giving practical help to people who want to stop smoking. Some useful pamphlets are available and the Quitline can offer advice and put people in touch with local support groups.

Relate
Herbert Gray College, Little Church Street, Rugby, Warwickshire CV21 3AP. Tel: 01788 573241.
E-mail: enquiries@national.relate.org.uk

Website: www.relate.org.uk
Relate is a charity providing relationship education and counselling. Overall 2300 trained counsellors work in 126 Relate Centres in the UK. There is an extensive list of publications covering issues such as male and female health problems, sexual difficulties, self-esteem, depression, and remarriage.

Vegetarian Society
Parkdale, Dunham Road, Altrincham, Cheshire WA14 4QG.
Tel: 0161 925 2000. Fax: 0161 926 9182.
E-mail: info@vegsoc.org or if e-mailing from abroad:
info@vegsoc.demon.co.uk
Website: www.vegsoc.org.uk

Australia and New Zealand
National Heart Foundation of Australia
Corner Denison St and Geil Court, Deakin, ACT 2600. Tel: 1300 36 27 87.
E-mail: heartlinesa@heartfoundation.com.au
Website: www.heartfoundation.com.au
Information on heart disease and how to quit smoking.

National Heart Foundation of New Zealand
National Office, PO Box 17160, Greenlane, Auckland. Tel: 09 571 9191. Fax: 09 571 9190.
E-mail: info@nhf.org.nz
Website: www.nhf.org.nz

Alcoholics Anonymous
General Service Office, Royal South Sydney Hospital, Joynton Avenue, 2017 Zetland, Australia. Tel: 61 2 663 1206 Fax: 61 2 313 8496.

General Service Office, PO Box 6458, Unit 4, Level 2, Harbour City Center, Panama Street, Wellington, New Zealand. Tel: 64 4 472 4250 Fax: 64 4 472 4251.
E-mail: nzgso@clear.net.nz

Nutrition Australia

Website: www.nutritionaustralia.org
Visit their website for details of your local organisations.

Dietitians Association of Australia

1/8 Phipps Close, Deakin, ACT 2600. Tel: 02 6282 9555 Fax: 02 6282 9888.
E-mail: nationaloffice@daa.asn.au
Website: www.daa.asn.au

USA and Canada

American Heart Association

7272 Greenville Avenue, Dallas, TX 75231. Tel: 800 242 8721

Heart and Stroke Association of Canada

22 Queen Street, Suite 1402, Ottawa, Ontario K1P 5V9. Tel: 613 569 4361 Fax: 613 569 3278.
Website: www.heartandstroke.ca

Canadian Association for Familial Hypercholesterolaemia – FH

Dr Roederer – President, 110 Avenue des Pins Quest, Porte 444, Montreal, Quebec H2W 1R7, Canada. Tel: 1 987 5740 Fax: 1 987 5741.
E-mail: achf@ircm.gc.ca

Alcoholics Anonymous

General Service Office, Grand Central Station, PO Box 459, New York, NY 10163. Tel: 212 870 3400
Website: www.alcoholics-anonymous.org

Centre for Food Safety and Applied Nutrition

Outreach and Information Center, Center for Food Safety and Applied Nutrition, 200C Street SW (HFS-555), Washington, DC 20204. Toll-free information line: 1 888 723 3366.

Canada's National Institute of Nutrition
205 Carling Avenue, Suite 302, Ottawa, Ontario, K1S 2E1,
Canada. Tel: 613 235 3355 Fax: 613 235 7032.
E-mail: nin@nin.ca
Website: www.nin.ca

Further Reading

Steve Biddulph, *Manhood*, Hawthorn Press, 1998

Collins Gem, *Calorie Counter*, HarperCollins, 2000

Stephen Covey, *First Things First*, Simon and Schuster, 1992

Patrick Holford, *The Optimum Nutrition Bible*, Piatkus, 1998

Patrick Holford and Judy Ridgway, *The Optimum Nutrition Cookbook*, Piatkus, 1999

J. Galloway, *Galloway's Book on Running*, Shelter Publications, 1984

C. R. Gillman, *Executive Fitness for Men*, Piatkus, 1997

Carolyn Humphries, *The Classic 1,000 Low-fat Recipes*, Foulsham Books, 1999

Carolyn Humphries, *7 Day Low-fat, Low-salt Cookbook*, Foulsham Books, 1999

Sam Keen, *Fire in the Belly: On being a man*, Bantam Books 1992

Sue Kreitzman, *Sue Kreitzman's Low-fat Desserts*, Piatkus, 1998

Sue Kreitzman, *Sue Kreitzman's Low-fat Lifeplan*, Piatkus, 1999

Sue Kreitzman, *Sue Kreitzman's Low-fat Vegetarian Cookbook*, Piatkus, 1998

Cathy Kyle (ed.), *The Complete Calorie Counter*, Pan Books, 1989

Sally Mansfield, *Low fat*, Reed Consumer Books Ltd., 1998 (available at Marks & Spencers)

Eileen Mulligan, *Life Coaching: change your life in 7 days*, Piatkus, 1999

Roshi Razzaq, *Indian Low-fat Cookery*, Apple Press, 2000

Sue Spitler (ed.), *1,001 Low-Fat Recipes*, Surrey Books, 1998

Sue Spitler (ed.), *1,001 Low-Fat Vegetarian Recipes*, Surrey Books, 2000

Judith Wills, *Judith Wills' Slimmers' Cookbook*, Piatkus, 1997

Index

Page references to figures or diagrams are in *italic*.

Index